Women Rule the Plot

AUGUST-SEPTEMBER, 1920.

Price 3d., Post Free, 4d.

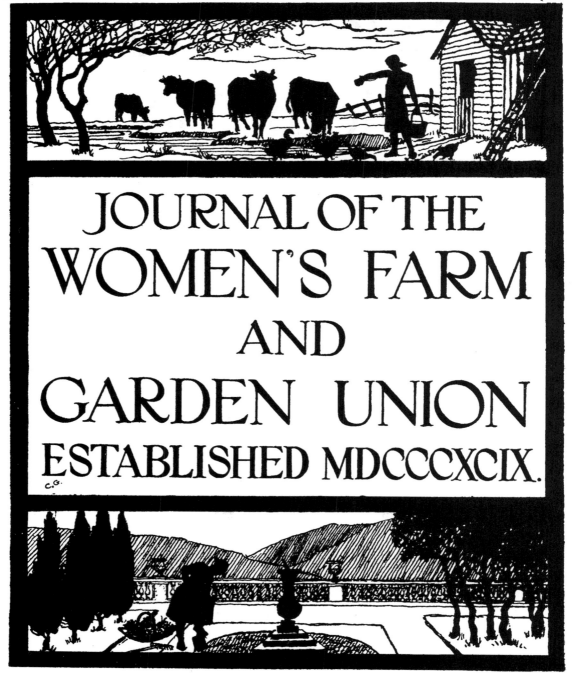

JOURNAL OF THE WOMEN'S FARM AND GARDEN UNION ESTABLISHED MDCCCXCIX.

The *Association* produced a *Journal* from its earliest days.

WOMEN
Rule the Plot

The Story of the 100 Year
Fight to Establish Women's Place
in Farm and Garden

Peter King

Duckworth

First published in 1999 by
Gerald Duckworth & Co. Ltd.
61 Frith Street, London W1V 5TA
Tel: 0171 434 4242
Fax: 0171 434 4420
Email: enquiries @ duckworth-publishers.co.uk

A catalogue record for this book is available
from the British Library

ISBN 0 7156 2949 2

Designed and typeset by Tony Hart, Isle of Wight
Printed in Great Britain by The Bath Press, Bath

Contents

Acknowledgements

This book would not have been written without the aid of Jo Currie, who introduced me to the WFGA and who assisted with much of the research, especially with the chapters describing women's place in English farm and garden over the centuries. I am most grateful. Others who have been helpful with background information about early members of the Association include Jane Beckett, Lord Bridgeman, Ursula Buchan, George Courtauld, Rev. Christopher Courtauld, Ariel Crittall, Sir Edward Ford, Lionel Jebb, Shirley Rodden, Joanna Smith and Lord Tweedsmuir.

Rory Stuart's article in the RHS magazine *The Garden* brought memories of the early days of the WFGA and WLA. Information about present-day members of the Association was kindly provided by those featured in the Epilogue and details about Mrs. Lancaster's garden by Martin Wood and *Hortus*.

Special help was provided by the librarians of the following: the Gertrude Tuckwell Collection; the Royal Horticultural Society; the Bodleian; the Oxford Central Library; the Royal Agricultural Society; the University of Reading; the Fawcett Library; the Imperial War Museum; Chelmsford (Essex) Library; Welling College; Moreton Morrell Agricultural College; Library of Rural History; Reading and Wye College. My thanks to them all.

It would not have been possible to complete the book without the help from Katherine Lambert, Wendy Turner and, at the WFGA, Margaret Spinks and Patricia McHugh.

Acknowledgement is made to Punch Magazine for permission to reproduce the cartoons on pp74, 98 and 115 and to Topham Picturepoint for the picture on p58; to the Tate Gallery and the William Nicholson Estate for the picture on p144, copyright Elizabeth Banks. The photograph on p154 was the work of Sarah Fitt and those on pp67 and 150 were supplied by Laurence Hill.

Finally, while every attempt has been made to establish copyright and make due acknowledgements, I apologise for any failure in this respect, and for any errors. These are my responsibility and not that of those individuals and institutions who have been so generous with their advice.

Many values in this book are given without any realistic present-day equivalent. The buying power of £1 at selected dates in current terms would be as follows:

1909	£35
1925	£19
1931	£26
1949	£13
1967	£7.50
1987	£2

Prologue

THE GREAT women's emancipation movement of the late nineteenth century had a hole in its bucket – it had done little for women working, or wanting to work, in farm and garden. Theirs was a man's world, and women had nowhere to go for training for skilled employment in agriculture or horticulture. 'Peasants' was the word that described most aptly the women who worked on the land.

Changes began to take place in the 1890s when the first female students were accepted at Swanley College in Kent, founded eleven years earlier to provide agricultural training to graduate level. Within a few years there were thirty-nine of them and by 1903 demand was such that all sixty-three students were female. Meanwhile belated progress was made at the Botanic Gardens at Kew, which set up a school in 1897 and allowed in eight women by 1901.

The 1890s are, of course, better known as the Naughty Nineties. The naughtiness started at the top of society, with leadership provided by the Prince of Wales, son of Queen Victoria and future King of England. In such a moral climate it is therefore a matter of some surprise that Edward's favourite mistress should be one of the most vigorous supporters of agricultural training for women. This innovator was none other than Frances Evelyn, Countess of Warwick, better known as Daisy. Prince Edward called her 'my darling little Daisy wife' and the general public sang about her in the ditty 'Daisy, Daisy, give me your answer do!' But Edward the Caresser (as he was known in his social circle) was already married to Alexandra so could not ask Daisy to marry him, despite the fact that she was his favourite among a sizeable army of ladies, all volunteers, who attended to the royal needs. She remained a favourite until well into the 1890s when the Prince was in his fifties. How could such a woman with a courtly background become so involved with farm education?

One of Daisy's long-standing interests was social reform. She had already set up a programme called the Agricultural Scheme for Women, which sought to encourage educated women to work in light farming, gardening and other rural occupations.

She waved her banner by means of a publication called *Women's Agricultural Times*. In 1896 she met another social reformer, Miss Edith Bradley, whom she appointed her confidential secretary. Miss Bradley was hyperactive and, as we shall see, threw herself into any project which might appeal to her employer.

Just at this time Edward was beginning to tire of his mistress and was searching around for a kindly method of ending the affair. For her part Daisy, though not usually discreet, was anxious to clear her name, concerned that someone with her past might become a social outcast – a probability compounded by the fact that she was a socialist and early member of the Labour Party, predilections not calculated to endear her to her peers. The rupture came when Edward met Mrs Alice Keppel, a lady of somewhat greater discretion than Daisy. The latter began to feel the time had come for her to make the most of her rural interests. In *Who's Who* she described her recreations as 'the encouragement of gardening as a hobby, of which she has published an interesting account', and mentioned *en passant* that she 'owns 23,000 acres'. In her autobiography, *Life's Ebb and Flow*, Lady Warwick claimed that rural education activities were one of her closest concerns. 'I have often thrown discretion, money and self-interest to the winds when I have been caught by the glamour of an idea [and] Education was always my absorbing interest.'

An ideal outlet for her new passion presented itself in the course of disengaging herself from the Prince. She wrote to him, in January 1898, a 'parting letter' (which, incidentally, she would later use in an unsuccessful attempt to blackmail him) to which he replied as follows:

> We must also endeavour to get up some object in common – some philanthropic one I mean – which may have a common interest to us both . . . Alexandra really quite forgives and condones the past . . . but could you, my loved one, for a moment imagine that I should withdraw my friendship from you?

Here was a challenge, *to get up some object in common* with Prince Bertie, *some philanthropic one*, which might just enable her to continue some form of relationship with him, now that his wife no longer saw her as a threat. Or at least, if that failed, she would continue to be able to move in royal circles.

She already had extensive property in Essex, presented to her at the age of three, and there was also Studley Castle, near Redditch, not far from her home at Warwick Castle, which could be used for a philanthropic purpose. Whatever these properties would do for the future, her present aim, egged on by Miss Bradley, was to set up a farm training establishment at Reading University. Her organising secretary (Miss Bradley's new title) set about matters in earnest. A report in *The Times* of 17th August 1898 shows how quickly she moved:

The Countess of Warwick is about to make an interesting experiment and one that is likely, if it meets with success, to have an interesting effect upon agriculture in England. Lady Warwick's idea is that it would be useful to form settlements of women in different parts of the country for the cultivation of the land and thus enable them to add to their incomes by the sale of fruit, flowers, vegetables, poultry, eggs, honey &c., the produce of their gardens and poultry runs. There is little doubt that a moderate means of livelihood can be obtained in this way, but in the present state of keen competition, success falls chiefly, if not entirely to the 'trained capacity' and organised worker. Those women therefore who propose to embark seriously in such an enterprise must first qualify themselves for the work. The [Lady Warwick] Hostel [at Reading University] which should open in October will be an institution where such qualifications may be obtained. It will be funded for the definite purpose of enabling women over the age of 16 to obtain a thorough training (theoretical and practical) in the lighter branches of agriculture, viz.: Flower and fruit growing, and packing for market, especially bush fruit, tomatoes, mushrooms &c., bee and poultry keeping, dairy work. The council of Reading College have consented to provide the necessary courses of instruction, and to recognise the Countess of Warwick's Hostel as a place of residence for women students. The grounds of the hostel will afford room for practical work. The full course of instruction will extend over two years, but students who wish to do so may join the short courses and special classes.

It is hoped that the inclusive fee for instruction and board will not exceed £50 per year. This will bring the training within the means of the particular class of women whom it is proposed to assist by the scheme – the one which has perhaps the greatest difficulty in finding a remunerative occupation – namely the daughters of professional men, left with, or likely to be the possessors of income varying from £30 to £100 a year. The sum of £2,000 will be required for capital and towards this amount some has already been promised. It is hoped that the balance will be forthcoming within the next fortnight in order that the hostel may be fully equipped at the beginning of October. Further particulars and prospectuses may be had from the Countess of Warwick, Warwick Castle, or Miss Edith Bradley, organising secretary, 60 St Georges Road, Warwick Square S.W.1

Life's Ebb and Flow also quotes her letter to the editor of *The Pall Mall Gazette*, W.T. Stead, a personal friend:

My agricultural scheme for women is developing well on one side, viz.; a hostel in connection with the Oxford University Extension College at Reading ... I have found a house holding about fifty boarders with charming garden for experiment. I have secured the support of £200 from Lord Wantage and the Huntleys, the Palmers (both biscuit makers) and Suttons (seeds) have come forward with sympathy and support and money, and we hope to start off at the beginning of next term with a dozen earnest students. I enclose a copy of my agreement with the college if it will not bore you to glance at it ...

Alas, her stratagems aimed at keeping on terms with Bertie were a failure. Her educational schemes, by contrast, had a good run ahead of them. Reading's hostels were at first successful enough, and writing to *The Times* in 1901 she claimed consistent progress, except for the difficulty 'that we cannot turn out as many students as there are posts for them'.

   With the demand exceeding the supply, Daisy moved her students from Reading to Studley Castle in Warwickshire and that institution, along with Swanley College, played a role in women's rural education over the coming years. Miss Bradley was its first organising force, designing uniforms, hiring staff, and working to have Studley recognised as a Technical Institute by the government Board of Education. Women of enthusiasm could undoubtedly do much for this specific branch of feminism, but the fact was that Studley College (as it became) was a unique exception.

This book tells a different tale, one of an organisation with some aims similar to Daisy's. Her Studley College has gone, while the Women's Farm and Garden Association, founded one hundred years ago, has, through the initiative of its members, succeeded in adapting to the great events of two world wars and social and scientific revolutions of considerable magnitude. To survive them, it had recruited some remarkable women and this is their story.

Chapter One

A Meeting to Surpass Anything
of its Kind

A HUNDRED YEARS AGO, women in Britain not only had no vote but little chance of a profession. A young girl would never be asked 'What are you going to do when you grow up?' because the questioner knew only too well that in most cases she would either marry or become a domestic servant. There were, however, changes stirring. An international working class movement aimed at protecting children and girls and to a lesser extent women had been active since 1840. Legislation in this sphere was introduced throughout Britain and the union movement began to involve women. At the end of the century an agricultural union for women was mooted.

The education and training of women became integral with this movement. Small groups of aristocratic (or at any rate upper class) ladies also set themselves up to make sure that women from all walks of life could be the equal of men. There were simultaneous efforts in Europe, America and the colonies. An International Women's Council was called in Washington DC in 1888, but its activities 'did not become a reality', according to the Marchioness of Aberdeen, a leading British supporter, until an international meeting was held in Chicago in 1893. Already national councils had been formed in the USA, Canada, Australia, Germany, Holland, Sweden, Great Britain and Ireland, Denmark, Italy, Austria, Switzerland and France. 'The movement is taking shape,' reported Lady Aberdeen.

Then, in June 1899, the International Congress of Women was convened in London. Its purpose was to hear reports about progress of 'the movement', listen to the counsels of women 'from almost all parts of the world on subjects upon which they were especially qualified to deal, deepen the sense of responsibility in women and promote a true sense of sisterhood and a high patriotism'. This was stirring stuff indeed, though a far cry from the mainstream union movement, which was more concerned with such mundane matters as working hours.

The higher social tone involved is clear from *The Times'* list of those who attended the inaugural meeting in the Queen's Hall in early May to hear the Countess of Aberdeen describe the agenda for June. In attendance were Sir Richard Temple, Sir Arthur Arnold, Sir John and Lady Swinburne, Sir William Wedderburn MP, Mr James O'Connor MP, Sir Joshua and Lady Fitch, Lady Marjorie Gordon (daughter of the Aberdeens) Sir Walter Foster MP and Lady Foster, Lady Newnes, Lady Joicey, Lady Stevenson, Lady Brunner, Lady Roxburgh and many untitled notables, not the least being Mrs Walter Crane and Mrs Beerbohm Tree from the world of the arts and Mrs Creighton, wife of the Bishop of London.

A fortnight later, when the agenda itself was published, *The Times'* editorial archly described it as 'of a somewhat alarming character inasmuch as it suggests an out-pouring of (chiefly) female oratory which is likely to rival even a British Association meeting in volume and variety. It is indeed proposed to surpass anything of the kind that has taken place in the history of women. Lady speakers from all over the world will expound their views or set forward their aspirations on almost every subject that concerns, directly or indirectly, the welfare of their sex.'

There were to be some sixty meetings between 26th June and 5th July. The number of papers read, or at any rate listed in the official programme, exceeded 230, but *The Times* 'hesitated to suggest any forecast of the ultimate number of speakers'. There would be five 'sections' to bring together those with like interests – educational, professional, legislative, industrial, political and social. Included in the professional section were subsections on agriculture and horticulture.

The meeting itself was held in Westminster Town Hall on 26th June, with sectional sessions in St Martin's Town Hall and in Church House, Dean's Yard. In addition there were social events — a reception given by Lady Battersea, a temperance meeting led by the Archbishop of Canterbury and a garden party at Fulham Palace, the entertainment at which was provided by the Bishop of London. A permanent secretary was appointed and offices rented in Victoria Street, Westminster.

Those who attended on the opening day included delegates from all the nations already mentioned and in addition from China (who appeared in national costume), Persia, India and Palestine. 'It might be asked', said the Marchioness of Aberdeen in her presidential speech, 'how in the world can such a conglomeration of [national] associations . . . formed for so many different objects, some actually opposed to one another, and comprising hundreds of thousands of women of different regions, different religions and upbringing, have an intelligible purpose and work together for a practical end?' Yet this was, she said, their main object in meeting together. Adhesion to the Golden Rule (Do as you would be done by) was the one passport required for admission to the council. Her words were punctuated by cheers from the delegates. 'It is often taken for granted,' she continued, 'that a congress of women should occupy itself in devising plans whereby women might be emancipated from the cares and duties of the home. But . . . this is not the ideal of this congress, for we hold fast to the belief that woman's first mission must be her home; that by it she will ever be judged, and by its home life every country represented at the congress shall stand or fall.' (Cheers once more.)

A speaker from the USA claimed that their own national council membership now numbered over one and a quarter million, a million of them women. As other speakers got down to business, the professional subsection laid out its claims that all girls should be trained to some profession, unless their parents were able to leave them an annuity sufficient for support; and that women should continue such work after marriage. Despite the variety of employment now open to women, much prejudice remained to be overcome; a woman trained for a profession would make a better wife than one 'whose teens and early twenties had been frittered away in amusement'. All sound stuff, although perhaps some delegates found the high moral tone less satisfying than basic advice about how to actually find a job. Day by day meetings continued on such subjects as 'international arbitration', the 'rational physical education of girls' and raising the school-leaving age to sixteen. Suffrage, naturally, was the subject of a special debate.

A meeting on 30th June at Westminster Town Hall discussed the potential usefulness of women as botanists. This was followed, a few days later, by two more substantial meetings of the professional sub-section, the morning being devoted to agriculture. *The Times'* report the following day read as follows:

INTERNATIONAL CONGRESS OF WOMEN

At the morning meeting the topic was 'Agriculture'. Professor Robertson (Canada) opened the discussion with a paper on 'Farming in its various Branches as an Occupation for Women'. Short papers were then read on the openings offered for the work of women in dairying, poultry farming, stock-breeding, bee-keeping, silk culture and ostrich farming. A further paper outlining the training of women in agriculture was introduced by Mlle Deleu (Belgium). Other papers were read on dairying and women's agricultural associations.

At the afternoon meeting of this section the subject 'Horticulture' was considered. The Dean of Rochester, presiding, said in his opening address that there was nothing so pleasant to the eye, moving to the ear, refreshing to the spirit and at the same time so helpful to high thoughts and quiet meditation as gardening. (Cheers.) In this country we were highly favoured in the matter of gardening because we were emancipated from the extremes of heat and were blessed with having an abundance of moisture from which we gained blessings in the form of rheumatism, sciatica, and chronic arthritis. (Laughter.) We had more gardens and more people gardening than in any other country. There was never a time when horticulture was so popular in this country as at present, or when horticulturalists were so determined to adopt the true principle of horticulture, which is the subservience of art to nature and not nature to artifice. (Cheers.) We were now beginning to discover the importance of allotment gardens and the county councils were doing all they could to promote school gardens. To make boys and girls into gardeners they must start early. With women as gardeners, they all knew the divine taste and power of management that was in woman's nature. He could not think of the slightest argument against women becoming gardeners.(Cheers.) There was nothing they could not do, and a great many things they could do better than men – in the arrangement of flowers, in hybrids and the production of new varieties. Where women had taken up gardening, as at Swanley College, it had been a great success.

This particular meeting would perhaps not have been notable had it not been the Congress's first to have as its theme the role of women in farm and garden. Twenty-two women were sufficiently inspired to decide, then and there, to form a national council devoted to their own discipline, and they went off to the Hotel Cecil in the Strand to discuss what its aims and objectives should be. Since the congress had been held under the auspices of the International Council of Women, which, as has been seen, had its origins in the USA, the word 'international' was a virtually obligatory addition to the title of the British group, the Women's Agricultural and Horticultural International Union. The word Union, incidentally, had none of the political over-tones with which it is encumbered today.

Following this initial meeting at the Hotel Cecil, there was a further discussion at the home of Miss Wilkinson, a well-to-do professional woman who later became the principal of Swanley College in Kent. Those present formed themselves into a provi-sional committee and held a third meeting in the autumn at 13 Stratford Place, the house of the Hon. Mrs Arthur Henniker, a supporter but not, apparently, a member. A council and executive committee were elected, the latter holding its first meeting in November. A prospectus was discussed and adopted by the council at its meeting early the following year. At one of these meetings, it was decided that the annual subscrip-tion would be 2s.6d.

Although Lady Warwick's appointee to the congress was a substantial figure in women's farm education and the warden of her new hostel at Reading, Daisy does not appear to have attended the congress herself. Indeed, there may have been some hostil-ity or rivalry between this new organisation and that established by her at Reading. Only three months later she held her own meeting – the first AGM of the Lady Warwick Agricultural Association for Women. *The Times'* report for 1899 shows that a firm attempt was made to attract supporters of the finest social standing for this new body:

WOMEN AND AGRICULTURE

The first annual general meeting of the Lady Warwick Agricultural Association for Women was held on Thursday, by kind permission of the Duke of Sutherland, at Stafford House, St James's. The Countess of Warwick presided for a short time at the commencement of the proceedings, and there was a large attendance, those present including the Duchess of Beaufort, Lady Maud Capel, Sir William and Lady des Voeux, Professor R. Patrick Wright (Glasgow), the Dowager Lady Westbury, Sir Philip

Magnus, Dr Kimmins (Secretary of the London University Extension Society), Mrs T.R.Seddon and Mr J. Marshall Dugdale, chairman of the association. Lady Warwick said that the association had been founded in February last with the object of helping to organise and direct the large amount of agricultural work now conducted by women – such as horticulture, dairy work, poultry and bee-keeping – as well as industries not necessarily agricultural. An influential committee had been formed and it was hoped to make the association international. They had every reason to be satisfied with the work undertaken by the association up to the present time. Mr Marshall Dugdale, who afterwards took the chair, said the agricultural scheme for women, requiring the building of two hostels, or halls of residence, for women students studying horticulture, dairy work, poultry, bee-keeping, and rural industries, had now been opened, and the question of opening a third one was now being discussed. The report, read by the secretary and adopted, stated that, from the letters and applications received, it seemed that the supply of women capable of lecturing, organizing, teaching outdoor occupations and handicrafts, gardeners, dairy and poultry women and bee-keepers, was not at present equal to the demand. The chairman moved, and Elizabeth Garrett Anderson MD [the famous woman doctor] seconded, a resolution in favour of duly qualified women being afforded the advantages of full fellowship in scientific and other learned societies.

Discussion then took place on the motion 'Future openings for women in the lighter branches of agriculture'. There was no suggestion, either from the group that grew from the International Congress, nor from Lady Warwick's educational establishment, that women would gain from entry into the more mundane forms of farm or garden employment – no back-breaking hoeing, no kneeling to weed, no delving with the spade. The emphasis was on the better class of woman who had already benefited from genteel and general education and who was now ready to be taught some of the finer points of agriculture and horticulture. Such ladies had already broken into university education. Though they could not qualify for degrees, there were approximately 300 young females at Oxford and Cambridge.

Why was it that women were now encouraged to take to the groves of horticulture rather than the groves of academe? It may have been because the women's movement generally at this time was anxious to do something essentially practical, rather than theoretical or academic. The tone is set in the first issue of the Women's Agricultural and Horticultural International Union's leaflet (15th March 1900), probably written by the journalist Mrs Chamberlain, who was also active in the organisation's newly formed employment department.

We now come to the opportunities for usefulness which seem to lie before the Union in the future. The prospectus states its objects thus: 'To circulate information, and to compare methods of different countries and districts. To advise as to training and make known openings for employment, and for disposal of produce. To uphold the highest standard of work, and to secure an adequate rate of payment for women engaged in any of the indicated lines.' The experience of the last few weeks enables us to add several others. For instance, we must aim at inducing those members under training to make their course of study as complete as possible. A fortnight's attendance at a dairy class cannot possibly turn out first-class butter-makers unless they are exceptionally intelligent. The pupils soon fall back into their old slipshod and unthrifty ways of working. We are glad to find that the Cheshire Chamber of Commerce has decided that the courses given under its auspices must be considerably prolonged. Then, as to the more cultured woman, who would perhaps not attend County Council classes, let us *insist* that she shall make herself efficient; and when she has done so, that she shall work and not teach. All want to become lecturers, and if this mania continues the lecturers will have to hold forth to each other. For the woman who has thoroughly equipped herself in horticulture there are splendid possibilities. Posts go begging now because the supply is as yet deficient of the right kind of women, rightly trained. There seems a chance also, that for educated women, trained in dairy work, poultry farming, etc., opportunities may arise, which have not been realised hitherto. But to secure such chances women must have definite, practical training, and at present the means of procuring this are few. Not only must the training system be thorough, but it must be entered into with thoroughness, not in a *dilettante* spirit, nor as a pastime to be entered into in a 'go-as-you-please' fashion.

Our present systems, in England, certainly leave much to be desired; to take dairying, for instance, the shortcomings of our own method of training are made manifest by the fact that Danish instructors have been engaged to teach in Ireland.

It is clear from this that it is the women of 'the educated class' who are to be encouraged to work in farm and garden, or, put another way, 'the more cultured woman'. From the vantage point of the present day, we should not label this as snobbery. After all, just as Emmeline Pankhurst would always dress up in the most stylish clothes from her extensive wardrobe before setting off on a suffragette campaign, so here the WAHIU ladies were putting their education, their professionalism, in a word their culture, at the forefront of their campaign.

Whatever their aims, it had to be recognised that amateurs rather than professionals still formed a majority of the Union's membership. An analysis of the first forty-eight of them by occupation elicits the following:

Founder Members of WAHIU by occupation

Amateur gardeners	12
Dairy workers	10
Gardeners	9
Landscape gardeners	3
Market gardeners	6
Farmers	3
Bee-keepers	2
Orange grower/Bee farmer	1
Lecturer (forestry & village improvements)	1
Florist	1

The Union was not put out by this. In a paper that she read at the Women's Institute at Grosvenor Crescent, London in November 1900, the indefatigable Mrs Chamberlain claimed:

Social movements spread from the top downwards. If, presently, girls and women of the less educated classes find that a country life, and work on farm or garden, is not without charm for the more educated classes, they will not be so anxious to get away to towns and shops . . . When it is seen that *ladies* are healthy, happy and contented working on the land, the rustic damsel will begin to think it may be worthwhile to acquire knowledge of the primitive industries they have so neglected.

It is clear that this was an upper class movement aimed at finding employment for the gentlewoman.

Chapter Two

Kneeling upon a Cushion and Weeding

IF THE LATE VICTORIANS were determined to change the role of women in gardening and agriculture, what was their motivation? The answer is in part that this role had continued unchanged for a huge period of time. It has been said that 'the history of gardening reveals sexism present through most of its length'. It was natural that women should want to see significant changes in this important area of national life.

In Britain, for much of its history, gardening and agriculture were one and the same – the earth was tilled to produce food, or, as in the case of herbs and some flowers, to produce medicine. Tusser, in his *Five Hundreth Points of Good Husbandry* (1573), puts it succinctly:

> In March and April from morning to
> night,
> In sowing and setting, good house-
> wives delight;
> To have in a garden or other like plot,
> To trim up the house, and to furnish
> their pot.

A medieval order of nuns would probably concentrate on the herbal and medical departments rather than

Women at work, fourteenth century.

Women milking and shearing sheep in wattle enclosure, c. 1340.

on food production, although even here gardening as an occupation was hardly distinguishable from husbandry. June Tabaroff, the historian of women's gardening literature, believes that this was women's traditional role, the ancient one of taking care of gardens and laying vegetable beds. 'We find it in the Adonis gardens of classical Greece', she says, 'or in the Roman custom of women tending the herbs.'

Nuns may also have been allowed to indulge in the cultivation of plants whose purpose was aesthetic rather than merely culinary or medicinal. We know that in the eleventh century the nuns of Romsey cultivated flowering plants and in the same period the Abbess Hildegard (1098-1179) from Bingen in Germany is reputed to have compiled a long list of plants known then, the list including trees, herbs and vegetables, but also ornamental plants such as the white lily, purple flag iris, rose and violet. The earliest English records of women working as paid labourers in a garden are probably the entries in the fourteenth-century rolls of Ely Cathedral, where women appear in the wages list for digging the vines and weeding. The number of later historical references to weeding women, or lowkers, is remarkable, as is the evidence that they were paid painfully little for their efforts. In 1516 women working in the gardens at Hampton Court were paid 3d. a day for removing charlock, nettles, convolvulus, dodder, thistles, dandelions and groundsel. Even ladies could benefit from weeding, according to William Coles in *The Art of Simpling* (1656): 'Gentlewomen, if the ground be not too wet, may doe themselves much good by kneeling upon a Cushion and weeding.'

It was not only nuns who took an interest in the cultivation of remedial herbs. Robert Burton in *Anatomy of Melancholy* (1620) claims that women were often more knowledgeable than educated apothecaries: 'Many an old wife or country woman doth more good with a few known or common herbs, than our bombast physicians with all their prodigious, sumptuous, far-fetched, rare, conjectural medicines.' In his *Paradisi in sole Paradisus terrestris* (1629), John Parkinson frequently refers to names given by women to plants, indicating their role in handing down botanical knowledge.

Such evidence as there is suggests that, taking the population as a whole, the woman's place in the garden was defined by her relationship to that superior being, the man. In Milton's *Paradise Lost*, the Garden of Eden is cultivated by joint venture. Eve describes:

> our delightful task
> To prune these growing plants and tend these flowers

even though, when the visiting angel Raphael was on hand, it was her additional duty to pick the grapes and crush them for his drink. Eve suggests to Adam that the solution to the problem of a growing demand for 'sweet gardening labour' must be to expand their family. At the same time she proposes that, as a couple, they work separately in Paradise so that their efforts will not be interrupted by Adam's propensity for gossip.

A century earlier, Antony Fitzherbert's *A New Tract or Treatise most Profitable For All Husbandmen* (1523) also puts the woman firmly into the vegetable plot, weeding.

And in the begynninge of Marche, or a lyttle afore, is tyme for a wife to make her garden, and to gette a many good sedes and herbes as she canne, and specilly such as be good for the potte and to ete: and as oft as nede shall reqyre it must be weeded, for else the wedes wyl overgrowe the herbes.

Barnabe Googe's sixteenth-century *Four Bookes of Husbandry* also refers to the garden as women's work:

> Herein were the old husbandes very careful and used always to judge that where they
> foundde the Garden out of order, the wyfe of the house (for unto her belonged the
> charge thereof) was no good huswyfe.

By 1617 the first garden manual written expressly for women appeared: William Lawson's *The Country House-Wife's Garden, Containing Rules for Hearbs and seeds of Common Use, with their Times and Seasons when to set and sow them*. This ran to a successful ten editions. He recommends two sections of the garden, one for flowers and the other for vegetables. The schism between the two types of garden is significant. In the next century it would culminate in the purely aesthetic landscape garden, with the kitchen garden banished from sight. There were already signs of this in the seventeenth century. Sir William Temple writes in *Upon the Gardens of Epicurus; or Gardening in the Year 1685*: 'I will not enter upon any account of flowers, having only pleased myself with seeing them or smelling them, and not troubled myself with their care, which is more the ladies' part than the men's.'

Flower gardening was also alleged to improve the female mind. Mary Wollstonecraft, whose daughter married the poet Shelley, pontificated in her *Vindication of the Rights of Woman* (1792), 'Gardening, experimental philosophy and literature, would afford women subjects to think of that in some degree would exercise their understandings'. Ten years earlier, Cobbett, in *The English Gardener*, had pointed out the 'moral effects naturally attending a greenhouse', which prevent women from indulging in dangerous pursuits such as reading novels or gambling.

> How much better, during the long and dreary winter, for daughters, and even sons,
> to assist, or attend their mothers in a green-house than to be seated with her at cards,
> or in the blubberings over a stupid novel, or at any other amusement that can possi-
> bly be conceived! How much more innocent, more pleasant, more free from temp-
> tation to evil, this amusement, than any other? . . . The taste is fixed at once and it
> remains to the exclusion of cards and dice to the end of life.

Vegetable gardening, on the other hand, came to be almost exclusively a male occupation. Writing in *Victorian Kitchen Garden* (1987), Jennifer Davies explains:

There would have been no girl apprentices. If a woman were employed, she would probably have been a weeding woman, paid a pittance to spend hours on all fours scratching weeds out of the gravel paths with spiked tips of leather gloves. This was in order that every path should be immaculate for the owner and his family and friends when they walked around on tours of inspection. Women might also have been given casual work, picking off caterpillars or hoeing, but it was a man's world and the god within it was not the master of the house but the head gardener.

Flora Thompson's *Lark Rise to Candleford* describes the division of labour in Oxfordshire during the 1880s:

The women never worked in the vegetable gardens or on the allotments, even when they had their children off hand and had plenty of spare time, for there was a strict division of labour and that was 'men's work'. Victorian ideas, too, had penetrated to some extent and any work outside the home was considered unwomanly. But even that code permitted a woman to cultivate a flower garden, and most of the houses had at least a narrow border beside the pathway. As no money could be spared for seeds or plants, they had to depend on roots and cuttings given by their neighbours, and there was little variety; but they grew all the sweet old-fashioned cottage garden flowers, pinks and sweet williams and love-in-a-mist, wallflowers and forget-me-nots in spring and hollyhocks and Michaelmas daisies in autumn. Women usually cultivated a herb corner, stocked with thyme and parsley for cooking, rosemary to flavour the home made lard, lavender to scent the best clothes, and peppermint, pennyroyal, horehound, camomile, tansy, balm, and rue for physic.

Farm work was also largely a male preserve. A survey from a farm population sample taken about 1770 showed that about 13 per cent of workers on farms in England were 'maids', though their duties were not specifically agricultural, nor were they the only category of female employed on the farms. A girl entering farm service characteristically did so between the ages of twelve and fifteen, with her parents' consent. Board and lodging was usually provided by the employer. Research suggests that such farm workers, male and female, did not stay with the same master for more than a year, and, once they married, women were unlikely to return to farm service until they were widowed. While they lived with their husbands on the farm, they would have formed part of the great army of casual or seasonal workers.

At key times such as harvest this casual labour force included many females. They were even to be found among the groups of migrating harvesters, particularly in northern and western England, where women performed a great deal of agricultural work on smallholdings. Women also performed heavier work in the harvest fields.

A report from the North Riding of Yorkshire says it was rare 'to see a sickle in the hand of a man . . . reaping being almost entirely done by women'. They earned 10d. a day for it against the 2s. paid to men for binding the sheaves. Later, as the sickle was replaced by the long-handled scythe, requiring greater strength and stature, fewer women were employed reaping; instead they became involved in other jobs, for example in spring activities such as hoeing and weeding.

Analysis of the census returns of the period shows that the number of women employed in agriculture, horticulture and forestry almost halved in the period between 1851 and 1911, although the total number of women in employment doubled in the same period. The signs are that women were increasingly unwilling to take up field work, which 'debased every finer feeling'. Hardy described this with his customary pathos in *Tess of the D'Urbervilles*:

The swede field in which Tess and her companions were set hooking was a stretch of one hundred acres, in one patch, on the highest point of the farm, rising above stone lynchets . . . The upper half of each turnip had been eaten off by livestock, and it was the business of the two women to grub up the lower or earth covered half of the root with a hooked fork called a hooker that it might be eaten also. Every leaf of the vegetable having been consumed, the whole field was a desolate drab; it was a complexion without features, as if a face, from chin to brow, should be only an expanse of skin. The sky wore, in another colour, the same likeness; a white vacuity of countenance with the lineaments gone. So these two visages confronted each other all day long, the white face looking down at the brown face, the brown face looking up at the white face, without anything standing between them but the two girls crawling over the surface of the former like flies.

This, all too often, was the cruel reality of nineteenth-century farm work for women especially – Hardy was here describing the 'fallen' Tess degraded from her earlier employment as a 'pure' dairymaid. Indeed the eighteenth- and early nineteenth-century myth of the female land worker as the dairymaid or shepherdess in 'sweet employment' was beginning to be overtaken by a more realistic appraisal. For example Charles Kingsley's *Yeast*, published and republished frequently after 1868, tore down the concept of a rural idyll, claiming that living conditions in the villages were not much better than those in town. Charles Dickens, too, wrote that field work 'converts girls into demons'.

These more realistic assessments of rural life began to be made just when the earlier depression on the land was replaced by what was widely regarded by the late Victorians as a golden age of British agriculture, with real earnings between 1850 and 1872 increasing by between 15 and 30 per cent. However, one should note that the census returns show a fall of 75 per cent in the number of female farm servants between these same years, although this may not be entirely accurate. The number of 'female relatives' on farms also declined over the period as a result of what the census authorities described as an 'excessive demand for female servants' from the newly wealthy middle class in the towns, when education was being brought into the countryside on a wider basis than ever before and when rural isolation was breaking down at an unparalleled rate. Hardy's fictional village, Mellstock in *Under the Greenwood Tree*, was based on Stinsford in west Dorset. In 1841 all sixty-three labourers registered in that parish were born in the village. By 1851 only forty-nine out of eighty employed came from the same parish. No longer were the villagers dependent on coach travel at 2d. per mile, even for an outside seat. Canals, railways and coastal steamers offered cheaper alternative means of escape to less backbreaking, better paid labour in the towns.

Then came the great agricultural depression, beginning in the mid-1870s . This was due to a number of factors and was increasingly to affect the lot of women agricultural workers as the century progressed. Prairie farming in America and Australia was developed along with the large barques to carry grain overseas. The cost of sending a ton of grain from Chicago to Liverpool fell from £3 7s. in 1873 to £1 4s. in 1884. Furthermore, secondary distribution costs fell even more sharply as the American rail network grew threefold in twenty years. By 1878 the Locke wire binder had doubled the crop of every prairie farmer. So, although European agriculture was far more efficient, it could not compete with the bounty of virgin nature. While cereal consumption per head remained constant in England, imports grew from 10 per cent of the supply in the 1840s to 50 per cent by 1875. Then, from 1879 to 1882, when there was no longer any corresponding rise in prices to offset the poor yield, came three wet summers and three disastrous harvests. The 1879 Royal Commission on the Depressed State of the Agricultural Interest could find no remedy. The total arable acreage in England declined by no less than 12 per cent from 1875 to 1895. Just to add to the farmers' problems, 1877 brought in a plague of rinderpest (the last in this country), 1879 saw sheep succumb to an outbreak of liver-rot and 1883 was one of our worst recorded outbreaks of foot and mouth disease. The first American cheddar arrived in England in 1879 and quickly saturated the market. (Dairies and dairy processing had long been large employers of female farm labour.) In 1882 the first frozen New Zealand mutton was brought into London on board the S.S. *Dunedin*.

W.A. Armstrong in his essay 'Flight from the Land' shows the following :

Net Losses By Migration From Rural Residues (Thousands):

	North	South
1841-51	159	284
1851-61	229	513
1861-71	254	430
1871-81	263	574
1881-91	349	496
1891-1901	237	423
1901-11	152	142

From 1881 to 1891 over two thirds of those leaving rural areas did not even go to British towns but emigrated, often to farming areas in America and Australia, thus adding to the competitive pressures on British agriculture. Only from about 1900 did prices improve, and with the steam traction engine having reached the limits of its ability to replace manual labour the mass emigration from the countryside began to halt. With this crisis, known at the time as 'the Great Depression', it was no wonder that pessimism was rife among all classes. At the century's end the general feeling was aptly summed up by Oscar Wilde's Lady Bracknell when she told Mr Worthing (who boasted of his landed estates): 'Land has ceased to be either a profit or a pleasure. It gives one a position and prevents one from keeping it up.' One result was further rural unemployment. 'Over and over again', wrote P.A. Graham in 1902, 'have I been told that the great secret of earning a profit nowadays is to keep down the labour bill.' Armstrong believes it was the reluctance of sons to follow their fathers on to the land that was the chief feature of the total reduction of the farm labour force, plus the departure of their daughters into service.

Let us now return to the role of women on the land in the last half of the nineteenth century. Armstrong argues that, as the century went on, the role of women was, to an ever-increasing extent, becoming confined to home-making. Another historian puts the reason down to technical changes: the sickle was ousted by the scythe and subsequent mechanisation continued to reduce women to more subsidiary tasks. A further reason was that they could earn more by other work such as glove making, which paid 12s. a week. Whatever the combination of causes may have been, there seems little doubt that by the end of the century the proportion of women workers on the land, particularly of single women, had severely declined. Indeed the historian Karen Sayer claims that by 1900 the number of women working on the land was 'insignificant'.

This chapter began by asking what had induced a group of upper and upper-middle class women to interest themselves in improving the status of employed females in farm and garden in the final years of the last century. In part this has been answered by describing how farm and vegetable garden alike had become men's worlds and this was, therefore, an area to be infiltrated. Not only were women conspicuous on the land by their absence, they were rarely thought of as experts, despite the expert work they sometimes did, or the knowledge and skills they possessed. They had not yet started to become trained, as men were, at colleges (there were none for them) or through apprentice schemes. Part of the answer must therefore also be the burgeoning women's movement for better education, for the vote and for entry into the professions (and other men's prerogatives) by way of recognition of female talent.

In 1897, Mrs C.W. Earle, the famous garden writer, visiting the women's horticultural college at Swanley, exclaimed, 'It immediately struck me as quite possible that a new employment may be developed for women of small means out of the modern increased taste for gardening'. A farm writer might have said the same. Here was a new source of supply – and there was certainly a demand. The men, however, would not easily give way.

Chapter Three

A Daring Experiment

HAVING BEEN DEPRIVED for so long of rural employment, ladies of a certain social standing now had at least three windows of opportunity open to them. The first, in point of time, was the college at Swanley, Kent, founded in 1880, surrounded by 43 acres of garden and farmland on which every aspect of agriculture and horticulture could be taught to the students, who were, by 1903, all women. The courses included 'Colonial and Domestic Training' presumably for those whose aim was to be sent out to colonial destinations. Miss Fanny Wilkinson, one of the founders of the Women's Agricultural and Horticultural International Union, became principal there in 1902. The daughter of the President of the British Medical Association, she had been educated at the Crystal Palace School of Gardening; the qualifications she gained had already enabled her to become landscape gardener to the Metropolitan Public Gardens Association.

Miss F.R.Wilkinson — a 'founder member'.

A second avenue for training, as we have seen, was Lady Warwick's college at Studley in Warwickshire, together with one of the similar establishments she founded for educational purposes. What she described as her extension college at

GOOD POSTS
FOR
TRAINED WOMEN

Train at Swanley College by
taking one of these courses :—

HORTICULTURE
Degree   ....   3—4 years
Diploma   3   ,,
Certificate   2   ,,

POULTRY-HUSBANDRY
College Certificate ....   I year
Preparation for National Diploma
     in Poultry Husbandry ....   2 years

AGRICULTURE
Small holders Course ....   2 years

RURAL HOME MANAGE-
MENT
Certificate Course for Teachers
     and others   ....   I year

SWANLEY
Horticultural   College
Kent.

For prospectus write to the Principal, Miss Kate Barratt. C.B.E., D.Sc.

Advertisement in WFGU journal for Swanley which had close connections with the Union, particularly in Miss Barrett's day.

Reading co-operated with Oxford University at this time, Reading having decided to make agriculture its predominant technical study. In 1898, the agricultural resources there attracted what their official history describes as 'a feminist experiment'. The historian of Reading University says that:

> this spirited venture, which enlivened our society in quite a number of ways and seemed to take the fancy of the Press, sought another home at the beginning of the new century.

It is not quite clear what this means, because it appears that Lady Warwick had acquired at least two buildings for her venture. In Smith's Directory of Reading for 1903 the following appears under the heading '*Agricultural Scheme for Women*':

LADY WARWICK HOSTEL – Founder Lady Warwick; Warden, Miss Edith Bradley; sub-warden Miss May Crooke.

MAYNARD HOSTEL [Maynard was the Countess's maiden name] – Sub-warden Miss Bertha La Motte. These hostels situated in the Bath Road were founded by the Countess of Warwick for training ladies (over the age of sixteen) in the lighter branches of agriculture, i.e. Horticulture, Dairy work, Poultry and Bee Keeping. The grounds, consisting of sixteen acres, comprise large gardens, lawns and greenhouses, vinery, mushroom house, potting and tool sheds; also a poultry farm, small dairy and an apiary. The hostels contain large dining rooms, library and common rooms, study, bedrooms, cubicles and bath-rooms, and provide accommodation for 42 students.

Thus it must have been during 1903, when the total number of pupils in Maynard and the other hostels had reached 225, that Lady Warwick decided to move to a sham

Miss Wilkinson directing operations, Swanley College, 1905.

castle, built of warm red sandstone, Studley Castle, near her own stately home in Warwick. The energetic Miss Bradley arranged the move for the thirty-three current students and staff before Christmas that year, and the castle was renamed Lady Warwick College. There may have been some continuing relationship with Reading because in her autobiography, *Life's Ebb and Flow* (1929), Lady Warwick wrote:

> While Reading University still laughs up its sleeve at what it has been pleased to designate a 'rich woman's fad' . . . Reading the University individually has shown such kindness, especially professionally, and the stream has begun to flow that will carry our students beyond the seas.

Lady Warwick's educational establishment was not as closely connected with the WFGU as was Swanley, but nevertheless this advertisement for it appeared in their journal.

The autobiography continues:

> Separation from Reading took place. A large staff of well-known lecturers was engaged [and] the Hostel has been concentrated on the 40 students in residence . . . One subject has been added which is bound to play an important part in the training, viz. The weekly lectures on business method, followed by book-keeping classes . . .

Although she made a public appeal for finance for Studley, it appears that its capital was largely provided by a loan from her husband who was a member of its executive committee.

Life at Studley must have been very different from that at the

Reading hostels which (the photographs prove) must have been rather grand, with a rose garden designed by the Countess, thatched potting sheds and 11 acres for practical work. There was lawn tennis and an active hockey club. As for the accommodation, Studley would have been cold and cheerless after the domestic proportions of the Reading hostels, where students could have a study bedroom (£88 to £126 per annum) or at least their own cubicle (£65 per annum). In contrast the Studley buildings had been badly neglected and there was no farm as such for several years.

The dairy students wore striped dresses, while others were kitted out in long Edwardian skirts, white blouses with stiff collar and tie. Everyone wore good-quality high leather boots which

Weighing-in, Studley.

'served well' in the Studley mud: some students bound their skirts in leather so that they could easily work off the clay. The students were inspected by Lady Warwick, who had her chauffeur drive her over from Warwick Castle whenever she stayed there. Alas, despite Miss Bradley's efforts, the facilities for training remained rather minimal – there was no government recognition, let alone greenhouses – and the organising secretary departed 'shocked and horribly upset' in September 1905. Her responsibilities were largely taken on by Miss Crooke, one of the sub-wardens, though she, too, soon left, setting up her own school of gardening at Ivybridge on Dartmoor. She was followed by a new warden, Miss Mabel Faithful, sister to the Head of Cheltenham Ladies College, who also only remained for three years.

In 1908 Studley College finally came into the control of a relentless pioneer for women's social reform, with visionary ideas of what that should mean for farm and

Curds and whey at Reading. Reading had been the original venue for Lady Warwick's training college.

garden. This was Dr Lillias Hamilton who remained at Studley until she was forced to retire on account of ill health in 1922. Dr Hamilton claimed that she introduced 'fun and enjoyment' into college life. Students ploughed with a two-horse team, and double-dug the clay while indulging in a 'fine spirit of comradeship'. They built their own boats to circumnavigate the lake, and made wheelbarrows and chicken coops. The word soon spread and in due course the English young ladies of Studley were joined by Poles, Russians, Swiss and Japanese.

Another window of opportunity, from 1900 onwards, was the newly formed

Women's Agricultural and Horticultural International Union. The organisation was, admittedly, one of slender means, but what it lacked in material resources it made up for in enthusiasm. It had little in the way of funds, no permanent office and no paid staff. The members took work home with them, and did not expect to be paid for it. The earlier founder members set the tone – they were mainly of the employer class,

In a Palm House at Kew where ladies were admitted for training with some reluctance.

specialists in their own fields (a farmer, an agricultural journalist, a landscape architect, an academic, and so on).

As employers themselves, the senior members of the WAHIU had first-hand knowledge of the poor wages and working conditions in rural employment. They were deeply concerned, too, at the lack of opportunities for education offered to working or even professional women. Miss Vanderpant, later secretary to the WFGA, recalled what she had heard from the pioneers when she herself joined the staff.

As far as I can make out everyone worked voluntarily. They had a good time because they had excellent people working with them, . . . all knowledgeable in some branch of outdoor work. Apart from the small subscription they had to raise funds from meetings held in various country houses and jumble sales. How did they get money to carry on all this work? It has always been a puzzle to me, but in spite of difficult times, it was undoubtedly by enthusiasm and co-operation.

Despite its somewhat ephemeral character in its earliest days, the Union took steps to assert its standing. For example, in January 1900 it was affiliated with the National Union of Women Workers. This was not a union in the modern sense, but 'a union of societies representing the various activities of women in the sphere of social improvement'. It was, said a correspondent of *The Times*, 'begotten from ideals', and was affiliated to a still wider organisation, the International Council of Women, which, as we have seen, had organised the Westminster conference in 1899.

The WAHIU was run by its own council. The names of the first members are not on record, but there is a list for December 1900 as follows: The Countess of Aberdeen, Miss K.M. Courtauld, Miss Annie Matthews, Mrs John Hopkinson. Mrs Fitzgibbon and Mrs Hoodless (the Canadian founder of the Women's Institutes in Canada) were also asked to serve. Mrs Tubbs was re-elected chairman and Miss T. W. Powell remained secretary. The council in turn was advised by an executive committee which, the minutes make clear, wore the metaphysical trousers. Alas the committee spent far too much of its time in the early years attempting to expand internationally as the American Mrs Emma Shafter Howard had wanted it to do. It also had delusions of grandeur, as evidenced by the desire at an early meeting to have the Princess of Wales as its President.

A letter was drafted by the committee as follows:

Madam,

We beg respectfully to call to your attention the enclosed prospectus of the Women's Agricultural and Horticultural International Union. We are aware that your Royal Highness takes a deep interest in all forms of out-door employment for women, and more especially in dairy work, in which your native country takes a leading place. We feel that your name would be of the greatest possible value to us, both at home and abroad, and we venture to request that you will honour us by becoming our President. It is the object of our Union to bring women workers of various nationalities in touch with one another.

Hoping to receive a favourable answer,

We remain, madam, etc. etc.

It was not clear if this letter was ever sent, but certainly the future Queen Mary never took up the proposal.

During its early years the Union was preoccupied with internationalism to the point of obsession, pursuing contacts and avenues in, among other countries, France, Belgium, Canada, the USA, Russia, Australia and South Africa. Although laudable, it meant that the committee was failing to pursue what should have been its main object: to increase British membership and raise income for local operating expenses. The plan had been that, as soon as the bi-lingual prospectus/leaflet was ready, 'efforts could be commenced with regard to forming foreign and colonial branches'. The leaflet had to include details of membership fees, and the committee introduced a 2s. entrance fee, in addition to the annual subscription of half-a-crown or life membership for £5.

From the start finances were extremely unstable. To save money the association held their quarterly committee meetings at each other's houses, but even so the secretary could only report income of a 'few pounds'. Soon expenditure far exceeded income, the main source for which, apart from subscriptions, was the advertising revenue from the newsletter. But as no one was anxious to advertise in a newsletter with so few readers, it was a classic vicious circle. By their fourteenth meeting, held at the

Grosvenor Hotel in April 1903, things were financially so bad that the committee decided to discontinue the French translation of the leaflet, on which they had ambitiously embarked, and to tell members that they would forfeit their status if they were a year or more in arrears with their subscriptions. Advertisements in *Country Life*, *The Country Gentleman* and *The Englishwoman's Year Book* were all considered, but this would have pushed the overdraft up to about £40.

The editor of the newsletter, the ebullient journalist Mrs Chamberlain, threatened, at a 1904 meeting, to resign if measures were not taken to clear the deficit, but the committee continued to set its eyes on international status.

The ladies of the executive committee usually took it in turns to chair these meetings and sometimes one or more of them would also be members of the rubber stamp body, the council. Mrs Allhusen, who had succeeded Mrs Chapman as chairman of the council and also attended committee meetings, requested a discussion on the 'gradual dwindling of the Union' at a meeting of the executive committee at the Southampton Place offices of the National Union of Women Workers in 1904. No membership numbers are available for this period, though from time to time isolated references are made to membership such as, at a meeting in February 1902, the fact that twelve members had 'fallen off'.

The executive committee had apparently felt that if they could somehow acquire permanent offices and a secretary, things would improve. The NUWW and the Women's Institute both offered space for £7 a year, 'to include a writing table and bookshelves'. This was not felt to be what was needed, so both the committee and the council continued to meet in each other's houses, usually quite grand establishments in West London, or, alternatively, at the Royal Botanic Gardens, Kew where Mrs Sowerby, wife of the head gardener, was the employment secretary. The AGM of the Union in May 1903 was held in the Botanic Gardens Museum lent by her and the newsletter the next month says that she 'still more kindly entertained the members and their friends to tea afterwards on her lawn'. (Kew had a long connection with the Sowerby family, with a James Sowerby providing many of the illustrations for the *Hortus Kewensis*, an ambitious beginning to a complete illustrated catalogue of all species begun in the late eighteenth century but never completed.)

As they continued to face a deficit of £40 or so, it must have been tempting to consider an alliance with one or more of the other women's organisations in their field. As early as 1901, pressures were applied by Lady Warwick to persuade the Union to merge with her own organisation, now busy getting Studley College off the ground. The ninth meeting of the Union was called to consider the matter and also to discuss how they should respond to a hostile criticism of the Union in the *Sheffield Daily Telegraph*. This had suggested 'an affiliation with Lady Warwick's Agricultural Association as the younger and least known society of the two and deprecating our existence as rivals'. Miss Chamberlain, acting as chairman, drafted a letter for the secretary to send to the editor 'setting forth our raison d'être and replying to the writer's suggestion'.

As the years went by, the distance between Studley and the WFGU widened, while closer links were established with Swanley College, where regular arrangements were made for the secretary of the Union to address new students to tell them about the advantages of joining the Union.

After the annual conference of the National Union of Women Workers in Edinburgh in 1912, the Union's newsletter contains an article by Miss Powell saying, 'We may congratulate ourselves that during the past decade there has been an increase of 229 women gardeners and florists'. However, an average increase of twenty-nine women a year into their profession seems little enough cause for self-congratulation. The committee was convinced that possession of their own premises, plus support from what we now should call 'the great and the good', would be the key to the Union's survival. They considered admitting men to the council. They proposed electing 'influential persons' as vice presidents. One of the latter was Lady Jeune who was to write that

trade is one of the many vocations in which women have embarked successfully, many women of good position having found themselves from force of circumstances obliged to adopt it and thus becoming the breadwinners of the family. But, owing to the education which, until the last few years, was thought sufficiently good for the women of the upper classes, it was extremely difficult for them to compete with anything like success . . . Fifty years ago the world would have shuddered at the idea of ladies becoming milliners, florists and dress-makers; today there are many well-connected and clever women in all these professions.

Oh what a lovely smock! The smock was the traditional gear for farm workers of both sexes.

These were sentiments close to the heart of Union members.

As for their organisational requirements, as early as 1903 a Miss Rutter was acting as permanent assistant secretary, and a search began for somebody for the more senior job. An employment department had been established under the indefatigable Miss Chamberlain. Since applications were increasing, Mrs Sowerby took this over, no doubt using her expertise as employment secretary at Kew. However an exchange and mart department was little used and was dropped. By 1906 the future of the newsletter itself was in doubt as the deficit remained at £40, and it was decided to appeal to the membership for one-off contributions. This saved the day and money owed to

Miss Powell, the treasurer, who had resigned in 1904, was repaid. The former chairman, Mrs Chapman, took over from her.

Meetings continued to be held in rooms in Ashley Gardens, Priory Mansions, Drayton Gardens, Lower Sloane Street and the like, despite the offer by Mrs Sowerby of a room in the Kew offices at a peppercorn rent of £1 per annum. The Union, however, was determined to remain independent. Miss Davies was appointed secretary at £12 per annum on a three-day-week basis. She only lasted a couple of months. Her successor departed even sooner, despite the fact that by this time the Union was exhibiting regularly at shows, particularly poultry shows, and the paid secretaries were being given a 10 per cent commission on income from entries. As the Union's activities expanded, the salary of the secretary increased to £25 a year. These activities were many – Mrs Chamberlain (now secretary) proposed a flower painting competition, entrants being charged 1s. each. By the autumn of 1911, secretaries having come

Cream of the crop.

and gone, as secretaries will, it was decided to engage one who would 'give the whole of her time to the work of the Union' and the salary of £1 per week was voted from Union funds, with Mrs Chamberlain undertaking to pay 5s. a week more to bring the salary up to 25s. a week – presumably for work on the newsletter, which appears to have been a sort of private venture by this energetic journalist.

By the following year, 1907, Miss Agar had become an active member of the executive committee. She was authorised to find a permanent headquarters and she proposed 'a very nice roomy office' which could be had for £25 to £30 in Queen Anne's Chambers, London SW1. These offices were in pairs 'and it would be convenient if we could find a lady to take the adjoining one to ours who could then answer the telephone etc.'. Members promised to provide 'pieces of carpet, a desk, a letter cabinet and a bookcase' and Mrs Chamberlain was authorised to buy other necessities for the office. All was made ready and the council were able to hold their first meeting there on 3rd April with Miss Courtauld in the chair. It was welcome news that since the previous meeting there had been eighteen new members and only three resignations. A further drive towards increasing membership came in July 1908 with an article urging members to find an official 'Correspondent' in every county whose objectives were to be:

1. To obtain new members.

2. To induce existing members to spread knowledge of the Union, to exhibit at its shows and to induce others to do so.

3. To keep her members in touch with herself, each other, and the Executive, so that it should be known what they are doing and how they are succeeding.

4. To sell Union papers, organise meetings, and to report these or any country events of general interest to the Secretary or editor.

5. To endeavour herself, and through her members, to influence less educated women, working on farms and gardens, and induce them to adopt the best methods.

6. To initiate some way of following up local classes organised by County Councils or other authorities, seeing whether the teaching was thoroughly understood and the methods of working practised continuously; not tried for a few weeks, and then discarded for the old, slip-shod, easy ways.

7. To watch the local papers for cases of unfair dealing with women producers, or unfair practices on the part of any such. To enquire into the cases, if practicable, and report (when of sufficient importance) to the executive committee, with a view to any possible aid that might be rendered or warning given.

The office at Queen Anne's Gate was not the only ambition fulfilled in 1912. However distinguished the council and its vice presidents, the Union had set its mind on having a royal patron. Their first thoughts had centred (as already noted) on the Princess of Wales (later Queen Mary) but, as Lady Jeune told them, a 'very useful rule had been laid down by the late Queen Victoria – that no member of the Royal Family should extend their patronage to any scheme that had not already started, and was in a fair way to becoming successful'. With no fixed address and a wildly fluctuating membership, the Union had, in its first ten years, been in no position to claim that it qualified.

Now, established in Queen Anne's Chambers, a stone's throw from the Houses of Parliament, their credentials were more respectable, and, possibly with help from Lady Jeune, an approach was made to Queen Victoria's daughter, Princess Louise, who had married the Duke of Argyll. The Princess was deeply concerned, said Lady Jeune, with the cause of higher education for women and had already shown her enthusiasm by her patronage of, and enthusiasm for, the Girls' Public Schools Company. She had also played a leading part in the 1899 International Congress (See Chapter 1).

The Union was able to point out its not inconsiderable achievements. By 1910, two committees had been set up (grandly called Departments of Employment and Education). Practical examinations in gardening were held at Hatfield House (courtesy of Lady Salisbury) and at Knebworth (courtesy of Lady Cobbold), also courses in poultry management. The latter were open to men as well as women and one of the first men to qualify was the poultry instructor at Wye College. Farms were lent for the exams in agriculture.

A handful of private gardening schools were well attended – one of the first being Lady Wolseley's school, established in 1901 at Glynde near today's opera house. Against this background of burgeoning activity in women's interests in farm and garden the Union stood like a bright band of distinguished sisters, distinguished, that is, not only socially but in their two specialist fields of agriculture and horticulture by such members as Miss Courtauld and Miss Agar. It seemed inevitable that Princess Louise was pleased to give them her patronage and so she did.

Development was now rapid. Two years later, at the meeting in November 1912, the hon. treasurer (Miss Agar, who had taken over from Mrs Chapman) was able to report that the Union remained in credit (just) and the secretary explained that since the last meeting twenty-one prospective members had applied, five old members had become life members and three schools had affiliated. There had been forty-one applications for posts and fifty-two vacancies on the employment register, of which twenty-five had now been filled.

What was now needed was a leader, someone who could devote her full time to the affairs of the Union, in particular their business affairs, and who could be relied on to do so for at least ten years ahead. Few appreciated it at the time, but the ten years from 1914 were to be seminal for the nation. They say that the hour finds the spirit it needs, and this was the case here – Mrs Roland Wilkins, first mentioned in the Union's records in July 1913, started to take an active interest in its affairs. In fact Mrs Wilkins knew a good deal about the Union long before this because she was, before her marriage, a Miss Louisa Jebb, and a relation, Miss S. M. Jebb, of West Hill Street, St Leonard's-on-Sea, Sussex, had joined it as early as 1901. Louisa's husband, Mr Roland Wilkins, a rising star at the Treasury, was at that time Private Secretary to Austen Chamberlain. We can be certain that Mrs Wilkins was to benefit from his advice in Whitehall corridors during the negotiations that were to take place during the First World War.

LOUISA WILKINS

In addition to the Women's Farm and Garden Association, Louisa Wilkins was a player in the Women's Land Army, the Women's Institute and, through her family, the Save the Children Fund. In addition she was a leading figure in the Agricultural Organisation Society (AOS) which played a seminal role in what is now the National Farmers' Union. Though she was well-to-do and able to finance her own work, her involvement in their movements had little or nothing to do with financing them and everything to do with her intellectual strength and organising ability.

  She came from one of those landed families and was described as being a member of the gentry, distinguished for intelligence, social conscience and a certain originality, the last being sometimes a synonym for eccentricity. Her father Mr Arthur T. Jebb was the squire of a handsome property called the Lyth, at Ellesmere, Shropshire, who had married a cousin, Miss Eglantyne Jebb, daughter of Robert Jebb from County Dublin. Louisa was the second of six children, four of them girls.

She was clearly a scholar, more reserved than her sisters, prone to melancholy but methodical with a scientific turn of mind. Early on she studied geology and took an interest in the home farm (later she was to set up a dairy there, selling her own butter, cheese and cream). The obvious place to go when she was eighteen was therefore the new agricultural course at Cambridge, where she could study (though not, in those days, achieve a university degree, as these were reserved for men). And so, in the teeth of her father's opposition, she went up to Newnham, where she was one of the first women to study agriculture (some records claim that she was indeed the first).

After completing her course she went back to live in a bungalow near the Lyth to act as her brother's bailiff for the home farm and specialise in dairy farming.

In 1905 she threw herself into the small-holders' movement, went to Denmark to study co-operatives, and travelled all over England (often by bicycle), wherever there were nuclei of smallholders. Her pamphlet on the movement, 'The Small Holdings of England: An Enquiry into the Conditions of Success', was regarded for years as the classic on its subject, and her lectures, which she gave around the country, were reported in full in the local press. Her interests, however, were not confined to smallholdings, but extended to the co-operative movement as a whole. She became a regular speaker at these Agriculture Organisation Society events and got a job on the head office staff in London, reporting directly to Nugent Harris (See p60).

In 1907 Louisa married Roland Wilkins. He came from a distinguished middle class family – his father was professor of Latin at Manchester University – and had a considerable academic record, crowned by a major exhibition to Balliol, Oxford, where he took a first class degree in 1892.

He made his career in the Civil Service, moving rapidly up the ladder. In 1899 he was Private Secretary to Mr Hanbury (a junior Treasury Minister) then for two years to Mr Austen Chamberlain, one of the most distinguished politicians of the day. He began to concentrate on Treasury work, being first, Private Secretary to the Financial Secretary and then, the year after his marriage, Principal Clerk to the Treasury. There were two daughters of the marriage, Sheila and Betty, but Louisa's duties as a mother did not prevent her from throwing herself back into her work with the AOS.

This interest in social affairs, the desire to campaign and the urge to write interestingly on the subject, were common to other members of the Jebb family, particularly to Louisa's sister Eglantyne.

She had gone to Oxford rather than Cambridge, then moved from Oxford to Cambridge, to study, amongst other subjects, economics. She too was interested in the smallholding movement, but her particular speciality was Cambridge charities, about which she wrote a book in 1906.

She had also joined the WFGA and the two sisters kept in touch with events in that organisation, too. The fact that Eglantyne's interests ran parallel to those of her sister was a major factor in Louisa's career. Both believed that a cause worth fighting for was the reorganisation of British agriculture to allow a more prominent role for women.

By 1909 Louisa was on the executive committee which produced *The Small Holdings Controversy*. This twopenny booklet, which had an introduction by the President of the Board of Agriculture, was aimed at a wide readership. It dealt with the problem of farmers or land owners who would not sell property though they might offer tenancies. The problem was, in Louisa's words, that 'the individual small holder is doomed to failure . . . He must co-operate or go under.' She begged the political parties to sink their differences in the common cause.

At this stage in her career, Louisa Wilkins had continued to impress those who (like the President of the Board of Trade) saw her as a woman not only of considerable business ability but also of exceptional intelligence. She may herself have believed that her sister Eglantyne had the better brain and this may be why, after 1912 when she became a Governor of the AOS, she arranged with its secretary, Nugent Harris, for Eglantyne to take over the editorship of its influential journal *The Plough*, a job she was forced by ill-health to give up in 1915. Nugent Harris's wife, who later herself edited *Home and County* for the Women's Institute movement, complimented Eglantyne on her work, particularly her regular articles on the co-operative societies. She was, she said, 'a personage who in a company dominated those present . . . by spiritual force [and] the simplicity of her goodness. She was selfless without a grain of conceit, but her work was well and beautifully done'. It must be added that she did the work of three people, 'manager, editor, reporter, proof reader, publisher, librarian and lecturer'.

The same might be said of her sister. It was remarkable that in 1912 Louisa was the only woman chosen to sit as a Governor of the revitalised AOS, all the rest being men of considerable distinction in agriculture. This was not a case of choosing the 'statutory woman' for a committee – no such thing existed in the pre-WW1 world. Her recognition was achieved on merit. Of course she had the advantage of a distinguished husband (Wilkins was made CB – Companion of the Bath – in the 1912 Honours list for his work at the Treasury) but it was her women colleagues and her sister who fuelled Louisa's drive. Even after they became too ill to visit one another, the two sisters kept in touch by brisk correspondence. For the last two or three years of her life Eglantyne suffered from a goitre which was associated with a weak heart; at the same time Louisa was in great pain from what might have been cancer. Louisa died less than a year after her sister, on 22nd January 1929, aged fifty-six.

Chapter Four

Highly Trained Women of Good Birth

AS WE HAVE SEEN, during the decade after its formation, the women who managed the affairs of the Women's Agricultural and Horticultural International Union mostly contented themselves with regular meetings at the homes of their friends, interspersed with hospitality at their own houses in Mayfair, Belgravia or South Kensington. They talked endlessly about international opportunities and occasionally a delegate was sent abroad to attend a foreign conference. There was a social chasm between those who did most of the necessary executive work and those they served (the membership). Mrs Chamberlain was one of the few who appeared to have bridged the gap between the titled ladies of the committee and the members who needed jobs or training, or both.

At a meeting of the Women's Institute, newly formed on the Canadian model and intended to forge a connection between women's life in the town or city on the one hand and rural existence on the other, Mrs Chamberlain bravely asked the Women's Institute (rhetorically): could women of the class who would otherwise be governesses, musicians, artists, companions or secretaries, become farmers, and would they be happy at it? Yes, she replied, if their tastes lay that way and if they were allowed the same measure of training as those in other occupations. 'We have experienced difficulty,' she went on, 'in getting for our beginners chances of obtaining secondary (practical) experience . . . Both in agriculture and horticulture this difficulty occurs.' All that friends could do was to take the students on and let them work on farm or garden under an experienced hand. 'They do not expect full wages,' she added, 'but are entitled to small ones, say 12 or 15 shillings a week.'

In a typical year, some sixteen vacant posts had been filled by the employment bureau, mostly gardeners, but there was one floral decorator, one poultry woman and three dairy workers. Eighty-nine letters were written in the first quarter of the year, and seventeen interviews undertaken. 'However,' reported Mrs Chamberlain, 'it will be seen that whereas only *untrained* gardeners remain out of work, it is a *small proportion of* trained dairy workers who get posts, so whether the supply will create the demand, or whether it is wise to discourage educated women from taking up this work, is a subject worthy of our consideration.' What she presumably meant was that those women seeking employment found it useful to become members of the Union even if they were only looking for, say, jobbing gardening work in London or its suburbs.

One member of the Union's higher echelons – Louisa Wilkins – had grasped the fact that the outbreak of war in 1914 entirely changed the ethos of the Union's training work. At the annual general meeting in December that year, held at that bastion of feminine education, Bedford College, she spoke out firmly about the need for more women on the land, and outlined the part the Union might take in war work. Few of those listening would have realised that here was a woman whose concept was to change the course of the war.

Perhaps the response of those members at the AGM seemed to Louisa Wilkins to be vapid – at any rate over Christmas she formed a ginger group and asked her friend Caroline Grosvenor to join them. With a few others they met at the Grosvenor home at 30 Upper Grosvenor Street. At what was described as a 'private meeting', the two were appointed as representatives who would approach the Union on a more formal basis to discuss how it might be reconstituted.

This meeting did not take place until 26th March 1915, more than six months after the outbreak of war. Three weeks later the council of the Union met formally to dissolve its executive committee, appoint a new one, and replace Mrs Chamberlain by a new secretary, Miss H. M. MacQueen, now called the organising secretary. It was agreed that the Union's name should be changed to the shorter, more informative and punchier Women's Farm and Garden Union, and this took effect from May 1915, although some members were slow to relinquish the term 'International'.

While these changes were being made in the Union's management and strategy, they continued with their day-to-day administrative work, searching for ways in which to expand their training schemes. In the summer of 1915 the Union's executive committee formed a Training Sub-Committee under the chairmanship of the Hon. Mrs Norman Grosvenor, with Lady Gwendolen Guiness and Mrs Baines to support her. The funds available to them were a mere £68 2s. 6d.

THE HON. MRS NORMAN GROSVENOR

Caroline Grosvenor was the daughter of the Rt.Hon. James Stuart-Wortley, a Privy Councillor whose family were the Lords Wharncliffe and substantial landowners in Yorkshire. Like most girls of her class she was educated at home, but because she showed an early artistic talent, she trained at the Royal Academy, where she later exhibited watercolours. Her brother, Charles, also artistic, had married, first a cousin of Anthony Trollope and then a daughter of John Everett Millais. He was a close friend of W.S. Gilbert and of Edward Elgar.

In 1881 Caroline married Norman, a younger son of the first Lord Ebury, a member of the Grosvenor family who had allied himself with a rich heiress from Georgia, USA. Ebury was uncle to the first Duke of Westminster (head of the Grosvenor family) and a great-nephew of the Duke of Wellington. His son, Norman de l'Aigle Grosvenor, was 'something of a gentle rebel' and regarded by his contemporaries as 'a traitor to his class' since, unlike them, he was a radical in politics, agnostic in religion, a friend of the noted philanthropist Charles Booth and William Morris the socialist, and a subscriber to the notorious *Yellow Book*. He composed a little music himself. His wife, tall and handsome, shared his views and tastes, some perhaps inherited – her mother had been a friend of the artist Edward Lear. In addition to her water-

The Hon. Mrs Norman Grosvenor, CBE.

colours, Caroline sculpted and published three novels. They were an ideal couple but alas Norman Grosvenor died in 1898 at the age of only fifty-three.

His widow (who lived for another forty-two years) was given a 'grace and favour' house on his family's London estate, first at 30 Upper Grosvenor Street and later 2

Upper Grosvenor Street, both in the heart of Mayfair. Amongst her friends was Leslie Stephen who brought his daughter Virginia Woolf to dine. Caroline also had an open invitation to her father-in-law's palatial estate at Moor Park, Hertfordshire, though she preferred the freedom of her house in London and the company there of her two daughters.

Later, her grandson (now Lord Tweedsmuir) remembers her sitting in her room in Upper Grosvenor Street dictating WFGU business to her secretary Miss Essex, 'who always wore a hat when typing'. Though her character could be described as 'artistic' she had a practical side, with knowledge of farming through the Wortleys, the Lovelaces and other relations who were large landowners. She was also an enthusiast about Commonwealth matters and inaugurated the Colonial Intelligence League for Educated Women, which had as its principal aim the overseas settlement of British women. This inspired a contemporary music hall song

A voice from the Colonies arrives
'Send wives! Send wives!'
The whisper floats from home's dear bowers
'Take ours! Take ours!'

Caroline, who had a keen sense of fun, found this amusing. Her more serious side is evident in her book *Memoirs of Lady Wharncliffe and her Family*. Early on she became a council member of the WFGU and was for many years its chairman. She held the office of vice chairman at the time of the Association's reorganisation in 1929, and her daughter Susan (who married John Buchan, later the first Lord Tweedsmuir) followed her as its president.

She was, in several ways, a key member of the WFGA network. Caroline was close to Louisa Wilkins whose youngest sister was married to a Buxton, and she had also spent time in the Middle East with Victoria Buxton. Another close friend was Meriel Talbot who spent her latter years at the home of Lady Buxton in Sussex. Caroline shared Meriel Talbot's interest in Commonwealth matters. And there was also the connection with the Gladstones – related to Meriel Talbot's mother, Miss Courtauld's companion and Caroline Grosvenor's own family.

Lady farmers at a fund-raising dinner.

They tried various methods of raising cash, as well as gifts 'in kind' from well-wishers. The later included farm hostels named by such distinguished people as the Strutts, the Somersets and the Guinness family. These started off in a promising way, and students were taken on at farms near Chelmsford, at another near Kettering and at Lady Somerset's property at Reigate. For one reason or another all of them proved unsuitable and the final blow was the closure of the Somersets' farm school at Reigate for reasons unknown.

At least two other farms are listed in the first report of what was to become the Women's National Land Service Corps (WNLSC) for the first eight months of its operation: Warnford, near Faringdon, Berkshire, lent by the Knight of Kerry, and Hocknold Hall, Norfolk, lent by Mrs Pelly. In addition there were farms or farm schools lent by the county authorities in Devon, Gloucestershire, Lancashire, Monmouth, Nottinghamshire, Shropshire and Wiltshire. Finally there were colleges which provided instruction at Cambridge, Derby, Wye, Sparsholt and Swanley. Apart from joining these institutional centres, another fifty-three members of the Union trained on fourteen different private farms.

At all these training centres, the students were initially under the sponsorship of the Union, but the WNLSC literature explains that, after their six months' instruction, they were 'subsequently formed into the Corps, as a branch of war workers on the land'. Of these a number were appointed group leaders or forewomen, and others heads of government training hostels.

At Mrs Wilkins' suggestion, a small number of trained speakers were taken on to

Wearers of the WNLSC green armlet would have preferred a more elaborate uniform – and eventually got one.

aid recruitment; meetings were called in London, large provincial towns and seaside resorts. To boost attendance, all hockey and lacrosse teams were circularised, and notices placed in the press. A colour poster was displayed in the London area. In a mere two months some 4, 500 letters were despatched from the WNLSC headquarters in Baker Street, all aimed at recruiting women to work on the land.

In June 1915 Viscount Milner had chaired a special committee to consider food production in England and Wales from the next harvest and beyond. His first report, issued with great speed, suggested that if farmers were to increase wheat production they would need the security of a guaranteed price of 45s. per quarter for at least four years, to account for the capital cost of turning pasture into arable land and of buying the necessary machinery for the larger harvest. The President of the Board of Trade, Lord Selborne, backed this report, but the Prime Minister, Asquith, greeted it, predictably, with scant enthusiasm – for the past ten years he had expressed no interest in the country's dependence on imported food. The final version of the report, published in October/November 1916, was far less radical and only tinkered with a few details of a completely *laissez-faire* agricultural pricing system, although it did stress *en passant* the need to organise women's labour on a more effective basis.

One of its significant recommendations was that a central organisation, such as the Women's Farm and Garden Union, possessing practical and professional experience of the type of worker required and of the best methods of training, appeared to be necessary for registering women applicants for farm work, superintending the training of suitable women and co-operating with the Labour Exchanges. Most importantly, Milner added that such an organisation might receive government funding. The newly reorganised, reinvigorated and renamed WFGU seemed to be beginning to work more closely with government departments and to be acquiring the official recognition that they had been striving for since their foundation and, most significantly, to be attracting financial support. This appears to be in no small measure due to the efforts of Louisa Wilkins. Perhaps her husband's knowledge of government priorities and government machinery made a powerful combination with her forthright personality and ability to put the Union's case.

Autumn 1916 saw a policy of price control for consumer protection and the establishment of the Wheat Commission, but any sense of urgency had to wait until the arrival of Lloyd George as Prime Minister that December. The Defence of the Realm Act set up powers for decisions to be made by the executive committees of each county's War Agricultural Committee. These WACs, introduced by Selborne in the autumn of 1915, were professional bodies, composed of seven members – farmers, land agents and the like – chosen by county councils and the Board of Agriculture. A special women's branch was formed at the Board, whose director, Meriel Talbot, reported directly to Lord Selborne. Meriel Talbot's power lay in (*continued on p60*)

MISS MERIEL TALBOT
(*later Dame Meriel*)

Meriel Talbot was what we would call nowadays a full-time quango person, and was to become one of the foremost women working for the government in the First World War.

She was born in 1866, daughter of the Rt. Hon. J. G. Talbot, MP for Oxford University; her mother Meriel was a Lyttelton (a distinguished family) and her grandmother was Mary Glynne, a sister of Mrs Gladstone, the wife of the Prime Minister. She was one of ten children and educated in London at Kensington High

School. The family lived in Great George Street, Westminster where it is recorded they were 'at home' for lunch every single day; anyone who turned up was most welcome. They were in London from February to July; their home for the rest of the year was Falconhurst in Kent, where visitors included Prime Ministers from Balfour to Baldwin. Not much is known about her early life, but in 1901 she became secretary of the Victoria League, an organisation founded that year, during the Boer War, to be an informed ladies' pressure group on the subject of Empire. Many similar women's groups were founded after the International Women's Congress, aimed to provide activities acceptable to those women who regarded the suffragettes as too radical but nevertheless wanted to have a political voice of some sort. Patrons of the Victoria League included Asquith, the Prime Minister.

Meriel Talbot travelled widely in what was then known as 'the Empire', visiting Australia, New Zealand and Canada in 1910-11 and South Africa in the following year. She took a keen interest in the settlement of British women in countries abroad, particularly those in the British Commonwealth, eventually entering the Civil Service to head a branch which encouraged female emigration from Britain. She may have met Caroline Grosvenor who was also connected with the Gladstones at that time.

In 1915 she was serving on the official advisory committee for the repatriation of enemy aliens and, after resigning from the Victoria League, she was appointed director of the women's branch of the Board of Agriculture, Food Production Department. This was at the time when, egged on by Lord Selborne, Lloyd George and others, the nation had finally woken up to the fact that it was food supplies that might determine victory or defeat in the war. Her work in this field was recognised in 1920, when she was awarded a DBE. She then retired to the family home Falconhurst in Kent, where she was known as 'the Dame', spending some of the time playing women's cricket. The Talbots were keen cricketers and Meriel had her own team. She was an outstanding batswoman with a fearsome cover drive, and was known as 'slasher Talbot' and remembered as a tip-top wicket-keeper. In her later life she was a member of the Royal Commission on the Police and a member of two important British Broadcasting Commission (BBC) Councils. In 1941 she wrote the first chapter of an instruction manual for land girls. She died in 1956.

the fact that she controlled the grants which the government wished to direct to the various feminist movements connected with work on the land. The largest sums went to the AOS, whose officers included Louisa Wilkins, Lady Denman, and Nugent Harris (these grants, from the government's Development Fund, were given annually between 1912 and 1923).

It was Nugent Harris who was largely responsible for persuading the government to fund the AOS to the tune of some £200,000, hoping to prime the pump of the co-operative movement of which, with the enthusiastic support of Louisa Wilkins, he was perhaps the greatest proponent. Many co-operatives were indeed formed and received help from the Development Fund – by 1914 nearly 500 societies had come into being. Unfortunately, whether because of the individualism of British farmers, or through lack of overall government support or of education in its principles, the co-operative movement never caught on over here as it had done in Denmark. Perhaps the greatest contribution made by the AOS, through its publicity and its journal, was that it helped to bring the plight of the countryside into the open and to produce a climate of opinion which eventually forced the government to do something about supporting agriculture.

Nugent Harris, whose wife was also a leading member of the women's movement, tried to use his influence to promote the activities of women in farming. He was not altogether successful, as he explained:

> For many years when Secretary to the AOS I tried to get the farmer members of the co-operative agricultural societies I was organising to allow women to become members, but I failed. Then I got two or three to yield. Several women joined, but we could never get them to say a word at the general meeting . . . I asked them why they did not say their say? They replied, 'We dare not because our husbands and sons would make fun of us'. I would not rest until I could establish some movement that would give the women-folk a chance to express themselves, free from the fear of being ridiculed by the men.

His opportunity came when he heard a speech by a Mrs Watt who had come over from Canada to urge the expansion here of the Women's Institute movement. The lat-

FARMER (who has got a lady-help in the dairy): " 'Ullo, Missy, what in the world be ye doin' ? "

LADY: " Well, you told me to water the cows, and I'm doing it. They don't seem to like it much."

ter had been set up in Canada by Miss Adelaide Hoodless in 1897. Nugent Harris at once saw an opportunity for a similar, broader women's movement in Great Britain particularly if it could be financed through the AOS, then flush with government funds. Mrs Watt, who had been secretary of the Advisory Board of Women in the British Columbian Department of Agriculture before she emigrated, decided to support him and urged the formation of Women's Institutes in the UK. Harris agreed to act as 'guardian of the infant movement'.

A sub-committee on Women's Institutes was formed within the Ministry of Agriculture (more of this later) and its chairman and one of its leading members was Louisa Wilkins. When it met in 1917, one of its first priorities was to elect a Women's

Institute chairman, and the favoured candidate was Wilkins herself. She had already made up her mind not to stand but had come prepared for this, and pushed forward her own friend, Gertrude Denman.

LADY DENMAN

Gertrude Denman was born not only with a silver spoon in her mouth but, it is said, with her bottom already seated upon a silver bicycle. She had the advantage of being elder daughter of the first Baron Cowdray, a man of infinite wealth who at one point appeared to own most of the silver mines in Latin America. She married well, her husband being the third Baron Denman and acting Chief Liberal Whip at a time when the Liberals, under Asquith, were in the ascendant. He was also Lord in Waiting to King Edward VII.

In 1908 Gertrude's mother used her influence to have her daughter elected to the executive of the Women's Liberal Federation. After two years of this she and her husband were sent out to govern Australia. Alas, she and Denman proved 'hopelessly unsuited to one another' and she turned more and more to social work at home. Louisa Wilkins recognised her friend's need to find a niche for the rest of her life and having first involved her on the WFGU committee then pushed her candidacy for the WI. This was no uphill task as Gertrude Denman had an AOS background and was close to Nugent Harris. Already she had started a scheme to make backyard poultry-keeping possible for the average woman, and had also set up a farm of her own with her partner Mrs Grant, which the two ran until Mrs Grant left for Spain in 1916.

Meriel Talbot, as director of the women's branch at the Board of Agriculture, also watched over the work of the Women's Institutes since, initially, these came under her departmental wing. She, Gertrude Denman and Louisa Wilkins came into frequent contact through the various committees of which they were members.

While Meriel Talbot was not an officer of the AOS she worked closely with it (probably from as early as 1912) until 1923, when its annual grants were formally handed over to the newly formed National Farmers' Union. She would also have known

Wilkins' authorship of the Board of Agriculture's 'Blue Book' on *Agricultural Education for Women* published in July 1915, her 'Report on Educated Women', published in the *Board of Trade Journal* in July 1916, and possibly her other publications on smallholdings.

Another colleague of these ladies was the WFGU member Miss Wilkinson, then principal of the Swanley Horticultural College for Women, who later also became prominent in the Women's Institute movement. Then, when Louisa Wilkins was persuaded to become a chairman of a small WI sub-committee of the AOS (a position she saw as strictly provisional), she arranged to have a few friends brought on to the committee. Miss Wilkinson and she also saw to it that Miss MacQueen, organising secretary of the WFGU, became assistant director of the WI. She had also formed a 'War Branch' of the WFGU, the Women's National Land Service Corps, egged on by praise from Lord Milne's committee on Food Production. This was to be 'a mobile force of educated women to help in recruiting and organising the work of women on the land'. As the government provided the WNLSC with a mere £500 grant, Louisa soon saw clearly enough that it could not, alone, perform the tasks envisaged for it, and so she pressed for the formation of a Women's Land Army. Thus the many roles of Louisa Wilkins and the WFGU at the WI, the WNLSC, the WLA, the NFU and the AOS can be seen to have come together in the period 1915/6.

To say this is not, of course, to detract from the efforts of Miss Talbot, who in January 1916 had been appointed Woman Inspector to assist in organising the Board of Agriculture's Women's Farm Labour Committee. She asked Louisa Wilkins to propose names of friends who ought to be co-opted on to the Women's Institute committee of the AOS. Through that year the general feeling grew (specifically in the mind of Miss Talbot) that 'the Institute movement seems likely to make a real difference in rural life' since there was a great opportunity for them as food producers. If this turned out to be the case, 'the Institute movement will be recognised officially' and be 'supported' by the Agricultural War Committees.

Miss Talbot went on a tour of Institutes (there were about twenty-four of them by now) to see for herself. When she reported back to the Minister of Agriculture, Mr Prothero, she told him the Women's Institutes were 'the right sort of job' and after ten minutes' discussion he had agreed with her plans. Fortunately the War Committee's support plan was dropped and, with some pressure from Lady Denman, the Women's

Institutes remained for a time under Meriel Talbot at the Ministry. Louisa Wilkins had put her weight behind this, writing that the Institute 'must be chiefly self-governed [and] the essence of the whole movement is democratic'. It has also been suggested that Louisa Wilkins put the proposal to Mr Prothero that there should be a women's branch at the Ministry headed by Meriel Talbot. Whether she did or not, that is precisely what happened.

Louisa Wilkins' efforts were rewarded. At the end of 1916 Lord Selborne took over the presidency of the AOS. He was able to do so because he had left politics following a disagreement about the government's Irish policy. There were, therefore, now three 'power-houses' at the AOS – Nugent Harris, Selbourne and Louisa Wilkins. Before many months had passed, the AOS was subsumed into the National Farmers' Union and Louisa had turned all her energies to training women for the WLA, using the WFGU as her vehicle.

There is no need, here, to try to disentangle the politics that absorbed the infant Women's Institute movement which did not, in fact, become the major food producer that some (during the war) had hoped it would. Both Meriel Talbot and Louisa Wilkins believed that, organisationally, it should operate outside the AOS, in part because it was clear that the large government grants given to the latter could and should not be used to subsidise the WI. One result of this was that Nugent Harris, a leading WI supporter, was rapidly sidelined. Louisa Wilkins, however, continued to work on the executive council of the WI (as well as on the WFGU) until the end of the war.

To return to 1915, on 16th March the Board of Trade had announced that it was compiling a register of women willing to undertake industrial, agricultural or clerical work. Already, a month earlier, Mrs Chamberlain had proposed a similar scheme in a letter to the *Standard*.

Sir,

WOMEN ON THE LAND

May we make known that we wish to hear from farmers, market-gardeners, and others wanting the services of women for work on the land? We can supply highly trained women of good birth and those, less taught, born on farms, etc. As well as some country bred women, hitherto working in service, or in trade, who now desire to return to the country, and will make themselves useful in any way on a farm to gain experience.

Applicants must state what type of worker they desire, what they can pay, and what are the arrangements for living. We have quite a good number who can and will milk.

I remain, sir, yours truly

(Mrs T.) E.L. Chamberlain, Hon. Sec.,

Women's Agricultural and Horticultural Union.

A Board of Trade notice, headed WAR SERVICE FOR WOMEN, which appeared in the newspapers in midwinter, was rather similar. Registration forms would be circulated through a number of societies (such as the Union) and, 'so far as special training is necessary, arrangements will, if possible, be made for the purpose'. Already a number of local councils had set up funds to pay for women's training out of the rates.

These government proposals for registration did not meet with universal acclaim. Workers' representatives themselves were suspicious, even after their unions had met Board of Trade officials, because it might mean 'a lowering of the standard of living of the working-class'. Further, it seemed to them that, having proposed registration, the Board had no idea what to do with the details of those who applied. 'It will not appeal to the best type of woman, who naturally does not want to pledge herself to she knows not what,' said one commentator. There was also the matter of pay – and this might mean that 'the patriotism of women is evidently going to be exploited to relieve the burdens cast by their patriotism on employers'. Some thought that women should resolutely refuse to take any work which men had done, for less pay than men received.

Finally, the Board of Trade had advised the union representatives that 'the classes' would in all probability be divided. A report from the union side noted that 'well-to-do women who have ordinarily nothing to do with their time will not be expected to mix with the lower orders'. The former would, presumably, be given the clean jobs and would probably donate what they earned to charity. But most of the women 'rushing to register' were 'women who do not need to work'. It was, perhaps, rather enjoyable for the unions to look forward to such ladies working in the place of a farmer's waggoner or cowman, but if, as was more probable, they took only 'clean' work, then, the unions believed, they should not expect men's wages.

Another contemporary report notes that, of the respondents, most women indicated that they possessed scant knowledge of farm work, making such comments as 'Am fond of the country and would be willing to learn' or 'Have been successful with chickens' or 'Used to live in the country and would like to go again'.

One man who saw an opportunity in this (frankly muddling) arrangement was David Lloyd George, the radical Minister of Munitions. In July 1915 he summoned the leading suffragette Mrs Pankhurst to his office to discuss who should allocate the women who registered to specific jobs. The radical politician and the militant feminist saw mutual advantage in appealing to women's patriotism. The pretence would not be that the government needed extra labour, but that women were being denied the right to serve.

Lloyd George put it to Mrs Pankhurst that what was needed was a big London demo, probably a march – the suffragettes were good at marches – to assert every woman's 'Right To Serve'. In fact the government needed to replace two and a half million men, required for the army, plus nearly another half million for the navy and the air arm, and it would help matters greatly if their female replacements came forward voluntarily. Lloyd George had already acquired about a million women, mostly for his munitions factories, and he was well aware of the need for more women to work on the land.

Some 30,000 women joined this London march, many carrying banners urging 'Use The Gifts And Abilities Of Women'. Such costs as were incurred in organising the march were paid for by Lloyd George out of his propaganda fund. As a piece of spin-doctoring, this episode has few equals. The *Daily Express* of 17th July 1915 commented in an editorial:

> The procession of women which is to take place this afternoon shows how far the nation has travelled in the past twelve months. A year ago a procession of women meant a demand for women's rights. To-day's procession, though organised by some of the women who were most prominent in the old campaign, does not promise any rights; it only asks that women should be allowed larger opportunities of serving their country.

The banner says it all. This march was orchestrated by Lloyd George.

Lord Selborne, that indefatigable campaigner for more effort on the land, had begun to set up women's War Agricultural Committees (WACs) as early as the autumn of 1915. Women brought in from outside the villages were to have special training, and he called upon help from the Union and from other special groups such as the agricultural section of the Women's Legion. There was little central control of these disparate units until the women's branch of the government's Food Production Department began issuing weekly labour charts for each county, which attempted to predict where the demand for labour existed.

At first Selborne's WACs had little effect; while they were given the names of women who had registered to work, they did little with them. The employers – the farmers – were, as always, suspicious of anything to do with the government. Early on, it is estimated that some 40,000 women's names were on various WAC lists but, as Viscountess Wolseley of the Women's Institute observed, 'in vain each day we scan the papers, hoping to find that the register, made many months ago, will at last be more vigorously utilised'.

While the registration scheme had been welcomed by the press ('the agriculture of this country can be turned over almost entirely to female labour', cried the *Daily Sketch*) the welcome was by no means universal. One reason was that the majority of registrations were from the middle class, and comparatively few of the applicants expressed a desire to engage in manual labour – despite the fact that the novelist Flora Annie Steel urged her sex to 'handle the spade'. There were some strange requests for specialisation – one woman wished to take charge of the animals at a zoo. The government had only itself to blame, as it had made a 'special appeal' to what it described as the 'well-to-do classes' or 'women of leisure'.

An analysis of registrations by *The Times* showed that farm work came only second in popularity to shell-making (2,400 women for farming, 3,600 for munitions), with 10 per cent of total registrations. But how many of these had a true sense of what working on a farm was all about? The *Daily Mail* had its doubts and quoted the following dialogue between two women who had rolled up in their motor cars:

First Lady: What will you register for?
Second Lady: Oh well, I suppose I can look after chickens and I would not mind the country in summer.

Fortunately, farming remained one of the rare occupations in which training was given. When the registration scheme was introduced, the Board of Trade offered free training at experimental farms for two weeks, and by the end of April 1916 word of this was so widespread that 50,000 women had registered . But when, in July, an MP raised a question in Parliament asking for details, it transpired that of the 87,240 now registered, only 2,322 had actually been found a job. The organisational avenues available simply were not working, and the employers and thinking public were not giving adequate support. The latter asked, 'Why should the ratepayers contribute to train farmers' labour?' The former wanted to know why they should pay 12s. a week for single female labour or 19s. for married women? The unions suspected that this was sweated labour and feared that when their men members returned from the trenches, there would be no properly paid jobs for them. The *Woman Worker* for March 1916 told its readers: 'Twelve shillings a week is not a proper wage for a woman . . . Why should women assist in keeping down the miserably low wages of agricultural labourers? No armlets and no "patriotism" ought to make women work at less than a living wage.' (Armlets were their only 'uniform'.)

Another factor was causing alarm in the media. It appeared, the *Daily Express* reported, that 'London girls are no good on the land'. It claimed that the Wiltshire WAC had found that 'when the girls come from London . . . their imagination is of lovely green fields, shady trees and, in the near future, a Colonial life with their soldier correspondent. But it all ends when they get to the actual life of the farm, with its mud, filth and clouds'. A Board of Agriculture representative gave the *Express* story an even more damaging twist. 'Most of the girls are of a "flighty" disposition,' he claimed. It seemed that the girls enjoyed life at the training schools but they did not like it when they arrived at the farms and were shown the actual work. They particularly disliked milking. Such criticisms came as no surprise to Louisa Wilkins. A year earlier she had expressed her disappointment at the lack of determined action to get more women, particularly trained village women, back on the land. They could be used on a part time Women's Institute basis, but they had to be organised.

Eventually, on 19th November 1915, she persuaded the Union to write to Selborne, drawing attention to the Milner Report of the previous summer, and in particular to the offer of financial assistance for a central organisation. The Union offered its services in that capacity. After this letter had been digested by Selborne things began to move along the lines of the original Milner Report.

A deputation of the WFGU, made up largely of its more active pressure group members, went to Selborne's office to discuss their letter. Present were Lady Gwendolen Guinness, Miss K.M. Courtauld and, of course, Louisa Wilkins herself. Mrs Grosvenor was ill and so could not attend. The outcome was that Selborne invited the

Union to submit a proposal outlining how it could help in organising a recruitment campaign 'to arouse village women as to the need of their services on the land' and to organise their training. This document, which Mrs Wilkins had probably already drafted, was submitted the following day.

A letter dated 1st January to Mrs Grosvenor from Louisa Wilkins suggests that she disagreed with Lord Selborne about some aspects of the new central body. He wanted this body to work with the women's divisional officers of the labour exchanges. She did not. There were only eight of these women officers and they had no regular co-ordination with the WACs. Mrs Wilkins clearly understood the shortcomings of county councils, who appointed WACs, and she doubted their ability get things moving. 'Where there is no competent or knowledgeable local person (and there are many such places) nothing will happen,' she wrote. She had told Selborne that, in her opinion, the only way to galvanise the WACs into life was to start a regular (centralised) recruiting campaign, where local meetings would be called, addressed by a non-local trained speaker 'with official sanction behind her'. She herself took on this role, and throughout the next year provincial newspapers throughout England were reporting her speeches at meetings of the local WACs urging recruits to the WNLSC.

Mrs Wilkins' letter to Mrs Grosvenor went on to explain that, after seeing Selborne, she conceived the following day the idea of a service corps or an army organised along military lines, rather than a mere metal badge or baize armlet to encourage recruits. Her rationale was as follows:

1. There are very few village women, if any, who can give full time service . . . In organising these part-time workers, it would be more satisfactory for the farmers to know that there was a 'gang' available rather than an odd woman or two for an occasional hour's work.

2. Working in a corps the women would be under the command of a captain or lieutenant, who could practically be a 'ganger'; i.e. somebody who could take orders from a farmer and see that the work was carried out. Amongst a lot of women not used to agricultural work, the farmer or one of his men would otherwise have to waste a good deal of time looking after them.

3. The greatest difficulty will be in getting the women to work at all. It is so serious

that every effort should be *made at the start* to hit on some method of making them feel *real war workers*. A Queen's Badge may help a little, but they remain individuals with only a badge. Corporate effort is only introduced in a case like this by something more appealing and sensational. No doubt where efficient local workers exist they will attempt something of this sort (e.g. the Agricultural Roll of Honour proposed by Mr Cowan, Winchester CC). My idea was to make it National, and so increase its prestige.

This letter shows that the new group at the WFGU, and Mrs Wilkins in particular, were the first people to see the reasons for the hitherto insignificant contribution made by women to the food production effort. Furthermore they proposed methods that would simultaneously help to overcome the objections of the conservative farming employers and improve the morale and prestige of women farm workers. Louisa Wilkins' letter contained the earliest written record of the term 'Women's Agricultural Service Corps'. It was she who conceived the idea of *something more appealing and sensational*, first a corps and then an army.

And an army must be paid. Selborne had apparently suggested that £4,000 might be obtained from Sir Lionel Phillips, one of the gold magnates from the Witwatersrand mines in the Transvaal, educated at Eton and Oxford. Wilkins, however, dismissed this proposal as 'not to be expected or even desired'. After all, she added, the Minister for Agriculture had admitted that 'this matter of woman labour in agriculture is concerning him more than anything else in his department. If by that he means that the food supply of this country is more dependent on labour than anything else, it is not the way to convince the Treasury of that fact by asking for £1,000 only'.

Sir Lionel Phillips of the Treasury had, indeed, been present at a meeting at Mrs Grosvenor's house just before Christmas 1915. Also present were Lord Milner, Lady Gwendolen Guinness and Mrs Wilkins herself. They had pressed Milner to approach Lord Selborne about the formation of a large central voluntary organisation. When he did so, early in the New Year, Wilkins and her friend Caroline Grosvenor went along with him. This time they proposed the idea of a Women's National Land Service Corps 'as a mobile force of educated women to help in recruiting and training local labour'.

Selborne responded favourably and seemed, to Wilkins' delight, to have dropped his earlier proposal to work through the labour exchanges.

Formal approval came in a letter from Selborne to Milner dated 20th January 1916, which suggested that he had adopted Mrs Wilkins' concern that village women did 'not realise the danger with which, owing to a lack of labour, our home grown food supply is threatened'. However, he went on:

> If under your auspices an Association was formed to help the local organisations established by the Board of Agriculture [the WACs] and to encourage the work by propaganda or otherwise by its voluntary and patriotic service, such an Association would have my hearty approval and grateful support.
>
> This is a movement which can only be successful if the hearts and imagination of our country women are so touched that out of sheer patriotism they will undertake work which may be so uncongenial and not highly paid, but which is second in importance only to that of munitions work.
>
> I hear that it is proposed to form a National Women's Land Work Corps for this purpose, using the existing organisation of the Women's Farm and Garden Union as a nucleus, and I have much pleasure in stating that the Treasury have approved of a grant to that body of £500 to assist in the training of women in agriculture and of an additional grant of £100 for every £1,000 which the new organisation is able to raise, so that, however, the total Treasury grant does not exceed £1,000. This, I think you will admit, is a real sign of the appreciation and sympathy of His Majesty's Government.

Mrs Wilkins, of course, admitted nothing of the kind. While the Corps, of which she would be chairman, had the go-ahead, the proposed financial support for its nucleus, the WFGU, was ludicrously insufficient. It was too late to hold up the formation of the Corps, and on 28th January 1916 it opened up shop in premises at 50 Upper Baker Street loaned by Lord Portman. Mrs Grosvenor was the hon. treasurer and Miss Crookenden was appointed secretary. One of their first jobs was to send out a circular, setting out its aims, signed by Rowland Prothero (the new President of the Board of Agriculture), the Hon. Edward Strutt MP, Mrs Wilkins and the Hon. Mrs Grosvenor.

The Corps' supporters read like a list of the great and the good, comprising not only politicians and leading aristocrats but millionaires from South Africa like Otto Beit, the railway magnate, and Max Michaelis, the mining tycoon. The object was to speed up recruiting, by providing training and funds to finance it. The scheme was inaugurated in the grandeur of Grosvenor House with the Duke of Marlborough in the chair, supported by Viscount Milner, Lord Rayleigh and his brother the Hon. Edward Strutt MP, Mr Walter Long MP and the two ladies, the chairman and hon. treasurer. Asquith, still Prime Minister at that time, sent a letter which was read to those assembled:

> My Dear Duke,
> I think it is of great importance that steps should be taken to increase the domestic production of food. I welcome the inauguration of the Women's National Land Service Corps as a movement which is likely to be very helpful towards the attainment of this object.
> Yours sincerely

The Duke, who described himself as one of the biggest farmers in England, said he was ready to support the scheme. Walter Long, not to be counted among one of Lloyd George's supporters, was more outspoken. He said it was no duty of farmers to criticise the women who were ready to help on the land – there were few jobs on the land which women could not fulfil. Lord Milner, when his turn came, supported the women from personal experience – he had spent much of his life in Germany where female farm workers were *de rigueur*.

Lord Selborne, who could not attend, wrote a strong letter, saying that the new body would use as a nucleus the WFGU, which had been granted £500 to assist its training scheme plus an additional £100 for every £1,000 they raised for themselves. In the final speech Mrs Wilkins said the new Corps had been formed to speed up the recruiting of 'all classes of women', though the target was educated women between the ages of eighteen and thirty-five. The government had requested that the Corps concentrate on women from urban areas for training as 'foremen' of detachments, as speakers and organisers. The Corps would keep the national register, formerly in the hands of the Board of Trade.

WOMAN POWER

CERES: "Speed the plough!"
PLOUGHMAN: "I don't know who you are, ma'am, but it's no good speeding the plough unless we can get the women to do the harvesting."

(Fifty thousand more women are wanted on the land to take the place of men called to the colours, if the harvest is to be got in.)

Within a year of its formation, the Corps had recruited about 2,000 women, who, after a six week training course on farms, went off to their new posts. They expected to earn enough to cover their living expenses though their pay was not to undercut or supplant that of local women.

The question was would the new Corps be any more successful than the Union itself – which it now enveloped – or the various other bodies which had attempted to get women to work on the land? Mrs Wilkins did not know it – nor did anyone else – but the war was only halfway through its terrible unfolding. Two years had been wasted in terms of enrolling substantial numbers of women to work on the land. Would the next two years show a real improvement?

The problem was that the best farm labourers had already volunteered for the army. By 1917 there were far fewer skilled men available to act as farm foremen than was normal in pre-war years. 'And with this decimated army we were proposing to carry out arable cultivation on a scale which had not been attempted for decades,' wrote Lloyd George. In an attempt to establish the aims of the Corps in the minds of the larger electorate, Mrs Wilkins wrote the following letter to *The Times* on 1st June 1916:

Two hundred and fifty thousand men have been called out of agriculture, and more are going. So far some 50,000 village women (and they are mostly part time workers only) have registered to fill this gap; and yet it is on these resident village women that we must depend for the bulk of the labour, because the agricultural industry requires scattered and not concentrated accommodation, and therefore cannot arrange for imported labour on any large scale. Some hundreds of women belonging to the professional and leisured classes have come forward to avail themselves of the proffered short war training, which will fit them to be full-time workers on farms. These women have proven that a strong, intelligent young woman without previous knowledge can, without injury to herself, take the place to a large extent of the less skilled labourers on a farm. Farmers all over the country are now asking for educated women. There is a special mission for such women at the present moment. Experience during the last few months has shown that women of this type, when carefully chosen and placed, have proved themselves invaluable, not only because of the manual work they do, but because they have been the means of (1) bringing out the village women in many districts where for various reasons they were holding back: (2) causing farmers who have previously refused to use the services of local women, who had registered, finally to avail themselves of this source of labour.

To put it shortly, one educated woman, by her mere example and encouragement and powers of organisation, has been the means of making available 20 village women, at the same time as she herself is also doing farm work.

As it is on the village women that we must depend for the bulk of necessary labour, the inference is obvious. We want more educated women of the right type to take this up. We want 2,000 women, not merely to work for 2,000 farmers, but to be the means of making available the labour of 40,000 village women. It is for this reason that I am asking for space in your columns, in the hopes that publicity given to this fact will enable educated women to realise that they may be the means of averting the danger which is now threatening the home production of food.

Are all our young women with no home ties really doing the work the country now needs of them? Or are not too many strong, healthy, young women engaged in doing light half-time work which could be done by older women, or women with home ties? If this is so, and if the need of the country is so great, has not the time come for their own consciences to comb them out of their present occupation? The Women's National Land Service Corps appeals for recruits to carry out this work. It arranges for six weeks' training at a cost of 15s. per week, including maintenance, and has free training to offer. Applications are invited to the Secretary at the Headquarters of the Corps, 50, Upper Baker Street, London NW.

It was from these beginnings that the formation of the Women's Land Army was to spring, making a major contribution to victory in two world wars.

Chapter Five

Your Country Needs You

L LOYD GEORGE always claimed that the food question ultimately decided the issue of the 1914-18 war. 'It was directly responsible for the downfall of Russia . . . and led to the collapse of Austria and Germany. Indirectly it was responsible for bringing America in the war through Germany's indiscriminate submarine warfare. . . Here in Britain, whilst we were short of shipping for imperative war demands, and our food supplies from overseas were becoming more and more precarious, we were allowing our own fertile soil to go out of cultivation.' Lloyd George added that he believed this happened because most farmers and landowners thought the war would end in 1915, so why should they waste energy and manpower on the harvests of 1916, 1917 and 1918?

By the autumn of 1916, food supply was becoming 'alarming and grave'. There was an increasing shortage of shipping. Eighteen months earlier Selborne had pleaded for increased wheat production and criticised a Chancellor of the Exchequer who refused to give the farmers guaranteed prices. On 30th October, as President of the Board of Agriculture, he had pointed out to his colleagues that wheat and flour stocks covered only four months' consumption. The potato crop had failed all over Europe. Land was going out of cultivation and labour was scarce. Matters got still worse when there was no shipping to bring in imports from North America; the Shipping Control Committee reported on 22nd November 1916: 'We are living from hand to mouth. In London there are only two days' supply, in Bristol, two weeks'.'

One of Lloyd George's first priorities on becoming Prime Minister in early December 1916 was to appoint a Food Controller to supervise production and distribution. The Asquith government had already agreed to this in principle. 'I do not believe there is a country in the world with so much good land that is not producing,' he said. 'In Germany, every yard of such land is producing food. . . .The second thing is you cannot cultivate that idle land without "mechanical appliances".' He wanted every inch of soil to produce food. 'I am told that there are one hundred thousand gardeners in this country,' he said, 'all skilled cultivators of the soil [but] you ought not to allow one of these men to cultivate anything that is purely ornament. . . . I do not believe there is a village in this country that ought not to be self-supporting.'

Lloyd George placed Lord Devonport in charge of the new Food Directorate, controlling food in all its aspects, a man the new premier believed had unique experience of food supplies. He was head of the provision firm of Kearley and Tonge and since 1909 chairman of the Port of London Authority. Rowland Prothero (later Lord Ernle) was brought in as President of the Board of Agriculture. He, too, had expertise. Back in 1887 he had published a book on *Pioneers and Progress of British Farming* and had briefly managed the Duke of Bedford's estates at Woburn. These appointments recognised that fact that, while munitions and men for the army had been the key factors for the first half of the war, 'the final event depended more on food than on fighting', as Lloyd George was to say. 'Food is at the very root of national morale,' said the premier, and while the combatants were deadlocked on land, sea power was the key to ultimate victory. The Central Powers could ultimately be starved into surrender. 'War is organised cruelty,' Lloyd George concluded.

At the end of 1916, one of the country's leading farmers told Lloyd George that the nation was producing less food then than before the war, and in 1917 it would supply less than it had in 1916. Large areas were going out of production. This only confirmed the new premier's own ideas but still, when he formed a coalition government, Lloyd George could not persuade his colleagues to take the necessary measures. So, in his first speech to the House of Commons, on 19th December, he presented an argument worth quoting in full:

'Now I feel that I must say something about the food problem. It is undoubtedly serious, and will be grave unless not merely the Government but the nation is prepared to grapple with it courageously without loss of time. The main facts are fairly well known. The available harvests of the world have failed. Take Canada and the United States of America. As compared with last year the harvests were millions of bushels down, and that means that the surplus that is available for sale abroad is diminished to an extent which is disastrous. In times of peace we can always make up the deficiency in any particular country by resorting to another. If America failed there was Russia or the Argentine. But the Argentine promises badly. Russia is not available.

Australia means almost prohibitive transport. When we come to our own harvest, which is not a mean ingredient in the whole, not merely was the harvest a poor one, but, what is still more serious, during the time when the winter wheat ought to have been sown, the weather was almost, if not altogether, impossible, and I do not believe that more than three eighths of the usual sowing has taken place. Let us clearly understand what that means. Let us get to the bottom of it. Unless the nation knows what it means you cannot ask them to do their duty. It is true to a certain extent you can make up by the spring sowing, but, as any agriculturist knows, that never produces anything comparable to the winter sowing.

'Those are the main features as far as the harvest is concerned. But we have also got the submarine menace to think of. Under these conditions, it was decided by the late government to appoint a Food Controller. We have actually appointed him – an able, experienced administrator, especially in these matters, and a man of great determination and force of character. He is assisted by the ablest experts in the House . . . the problem is a double one: it is one of distribution and of production. In respect of both, we must call upon the people of this country to make real sacrifices, but it is essential, when we do so, that the sacrifices should be equal: the over-consumption by the affluent must not be allowed to create a shortage for the less well-to-do. I am sure that we can depend upon men and women of all conditions . . . to play the game. Any sort of concealment hurts the nation. It hurts it when it is fighting for its life. Therefore we must appeal to the nation as a whole – without the help of the whole nation we can accomplish nothing – to assist us to distribute our resources in such a way that there shall be no man, woman or child who will be suffering from hunger because someone else has been getting too much.

'When you come to production, every available square yard must be made to produce food. The labour available for tillage should not be turned to mere ornamental purposes until the food necessities of this country have been adequately safeguarded. The best use must be made of land and of labour to increase the food supplies of this country, corn, potatoes, and all kinds of food products. All those who have the opportunity must feel it is their duty to the State to assist in contributing to the common stock, upon which everybody can draw. . . . There are hundreds of thousands who have given their lives, there are millions who have given up their comfortable homes and exchanged them for a daily communion with death; multitudes have given up those whom they love best. Let the nation as a whole place its comforts, its luxuries, its indulgences, its elegance on a national altar consecrated by such sacrifices as these men have made. Let us proclaim during the war, a national Lent . . .'

In fact it was too late to prepare new ground for the spring harvest of the following year. There was a shortage of fertilisers, feeding-stuffs and tractors (the country relied on their import from America). Furthermore there was a lack of labour, due to the fact that so many skilled farm workers had been recruited in earlier years. In January 1917, the Board of Agriculture was given special powers to take over land which was not cultivated properly, by the Cultivation of Lands Order. The new Food Directorate took over the supply of labour, machinery and fertilisers. Minimum prices for wheat, oats and potatoes were set by the government. A guaranteed weekly wage of 25s. went with the guaranteed prices. Lloyd George concluded his speech with an appeal which called forth all his powers of rhetoric: 'I want the country to know that our food stocks are low, alarmingly low – lower than they have ever been within recollection . . . It is essential therefore, for the safety of the nation . . . that we should put forth every effort to increase production for this year's harvest and the next, and that we should do it immediately.'

Here was a call that the women of the Union and their friends in the Corps could not resist. Hitherto, their motivation had been to improve the lot of their sex by giving them a profession. Now, it was a call from their nation, comparable to Kitchener's call the previous year to their menfolk, which went direct to their heads and hearts. The most startling development at the turn of the year 1915-16 before Lloyd George's take-over had been the move towards compulsory military service. This was not due to any shortage of manpower. On the contrary, more volunteers were still coming forward than could be equipped. The aim was to give the people the impression that the government was doing something active to aid the war – conscription seemed to them to be the answer. In January 1916 the second Defence of the Realm Act introduced compulsory service for single men. Voluntary recruiting stopped – but the call-up proved disappointing. Instead of revealing 650,000 shirkers, as forecast, it produced a million and half claims for exemption from essential workers like farmers.

At the beginning of 1917, the War Office notified Mr Neville Chamberlain, the new

Director of National Service, that it must have some 30,000 men recruited from the agricultural sector for service in France. Lloyd George, of course, wanted these men for his food creation programme. The War Cabinet agreed that they would try to find substitutes for the farm recruits from Home Defence Units, and that they would withdraw men from gardening and similar occupations. Once more they would try and secure women to replace the lost men.

The War Office reluctantly agreed that the need for increased food production was much more urgent than the need to build those large defence units which had been put in place to fend off a German invasion of England. Another source available to Lloyd George was the large number of German prisoners of war. After a few initial difficulties this proved most satisfactory. But, in his *War Memoirs*, Lloyd George wrote that the recruit

who attracted the liveliest interest was undoubtedly the land girl. Her aid, too, was at first pressed on the farmers in the teeth of a good deal of sluggish and bantering prejudice and opposition. When, in 1915, the Board of Agriculture tried to induce the farming community to employ female labour – 'the lilac sunbonnet brigade' as they were jocularly hailed in some quarters – it met with very little success. There was of course work that had long been done by women on family farms – milking, butter-making, poultry-keeping, haymaking and the like. But the idea that women could do the ordinary work of a farm called forth bucolic guffaws. This crude merriment roused the ire of the sex, and when a member of the Launceston (Cornwall) Board of Guardians publicly declared that women could not do certain forms of farm work, they challenged his statement in the Press, and eight competitors turned up at a public demonstration at which they efficiently carried out all the major operations of a farm. This was in March, 1916, and it aroused such interest that a month later a county demonstration was held in Truro, where 43 female competitors appeared and performed seven types of farm work, including harnessing and driving horses in wagons, ploughing, manure spreading and potato planting. The work chosen as a test was all of a kind only to be performed by skilled and sturdy labourers. One of the judges wrote afterwards: 'Some of the work was very well done indeed. The dung spreading and planting was excellent; and the way in which several of the competi-

Flax pullers.

tors handled the horses on the harrowing and in the wagons was a surprise to many of the spectators . . . I should like to see some of the men who have been cheaply sneering at the ploughing have a try themselves.'

When national conscription was announced at the end of 1916, Louisa Wilkins immediately saw that her Corps would be unable to meet the demands now made upon it and wrote a confidential report estimating that an additional 40,000 women were needed which it could not supply. Her Scheme for the *Organisation of Women's Service on the Land* put forward by the WNLSC summarised concisely the shortage of agricultural labour when 300,000 men were called up and analysed the ways of making up the deficit as follows:

German Prisoners	20,000
Interned Aliens	5,000
Conscientious Objectors	1,000
Older men from other industries	5,000
Farmers now working themselves	24,000
Part-time village women already registered	60,000
Released by using machinery	5,000
Total	120,000
Deficit	180,000

The report went on to outline the importance of state recognition, the method of dividing the country into areas, each area comprising large towns for recruitment, the desirability of each area having farm centres for training. Selection committees should insist amongst other things on medical examinations. Farmers should be charged fixed fees, payable to the farm centres, and workers should be 'paid as soldiers': board and lodging should be provided: workers should join up for a specific period and become entitled to increased pay as they gained promotion. Women used in this way were likely to draw village women in by force of their example.

The report did not shrink from describing the difficulties of getting educated women to work and live in isolated farms, of convincing them that this scheme was of vital and national importance, of improving present conditions of pay and work, of continuity of employment, of eliminating the unfit and of maintaining a sufficient supply of trained hands to meet new demands as they arose.

Mrs Wilkins now formed a small committee to put forward proposals for a recruiting and propaganda campaign. The timing was impeccable. There was favourable coverage about the efforts of women in provincial newspapers all over England: the following examples are taken from 1916. The *Daily News* of Warwickshire wrote of

'The Khaki Girl on the Land, enjoying health and happiness and good work' in the vale of Evesham where seventy girls referred to as 'Brownies' were working on a farm at Dunnington Heath. A Mrs Crozier, the wife of a naval officer, was 'Captain'. These women were part of an organisation called the National Land Council, described in the article as the 'only women-on-the-land enterprise in which the girls live a communal life much like that of a soldier in the field'.

The indefatigable Louisa Wilkins, often seconded by the appropriately named Miss Image from the Board of Trade, travelled countrywide to meetings organised by the local WACs extolling the benefits of the properly trained girls of the WNLSC and luring women to take up jobs on the land. The *Buckinghamshire Herald* wrote of a meeting of the local WAC attended by Mrs Wilkins and the Hon. Mrs Grosvenor. Mrs Wilkins described the work of the WNLSC as 'to act as the connecting link between the farmers and the registered workers . . . As to the work that women should be asked to do, she would say every job on the farm except such as involved heavy lifting. With stout hearts, short skirts and strong boots, they could manage most other jobs'. Mr Acland from the Food Production Department told the newspaper that 'the previous week they had reached the danger point in food production, and it was the women's duty to do what they could to keep production up'. The *East Anglian Daily Times* had published an article on 'What Essex is Doing', based on a visit by Mrs Wilkins explaining in detail the proposals of the WNLSC. She claimed 'Lord Selborne had put the matter very clearly before them by saying women of every class must assist – the squire's wife, and the parson's and the farmer's and the wife and daughters of the labourer . . . women should be appealed to on patriotic grounds, not merely as paid workers, although they must be paid fair wages'.

Meriel Talbot also played her part in the publicity campaign. The *Peterborough Gazette* reports a meeting at Northampton Town Hall attended by local farmers at which Miss Talbot claimed 'As many suitable women who could be obtained were required to help the farmers increase production of food in this country. Suitability was important, and women must realise that farm work was hard work . . . It was hoped to make the work of the Land Army women and the village women still more effective by arranging longer courses of instruction next winter.' Her words make it clear that, at last, the government wanted to take a 'long view' of the need for women's labour.

Chapter Six

The Land Army in the Field

JUST BEFORE CHRISTMAS 1916 Mrs Wilkins and a deputation from the Corps went to the Board of Agriculture to meet Rowland Prothero, a few days after he became its new President. They recommended two alternative proposals: (a) a Government Land Army on semi-military lines or (b) a continuation of the Corps on voluntary lines but greatly enlarged. Although some of the details of their scheme were not accepted, Prothero did like the idea of a Women's Land Army and set about seeing that it was formed.

His first step was to accept Mrs Wilkins' proposal for a women's branch at the Board of Agriculture with a woman at its head – a proposal put to him at a meeting on 2nd January 1917. Within two weeks he had reached an agreement with Meriel Talbot, who, as we have seen, a year earlier had been appointed the Board's first woman inspector. Under her as Director, the women's branch of the Board was quickly established, employing women only, though it was soon transferred to the Food Production Department. In March 1917 the WLA issued its first appeal for recruits aimed at finding 10,000 new workers. In fact, 30,000 applied, of whom only 2,000 had been placed on farms by the middle of July.

These Land Army women differed in a number of ways from those Mrs Wilkins had recruited to the Corps. The WLA was not confined to 'educated women' though the Union said, in its report for December 1917, that it had 'been specially asked by the government to recruit and train women of the professional classes,' such women being needed 'to serve as officers to lead detachments of workers'. Recruits had to sign up for the duration of the war (this was later changed to a six or twelve month commitment) and be prepared to work wherever they were sent. They could not leave their job without approval from the local WAC. A free uniform was issued and an agreed wage-scale was laid down. There was free travel to the place of employment and free training. The Union had been recognised as the central voluntary body for organising such training – either directly on farms lent to it for the purpose or, indirectly, by arrangement with farmers who were willing to provide short courses for new recruits. Training on farms lent to the Union was supervised by the farm bailiff and a lady superintendent provided by the Union. It was free, but living expenses amounting to about 25s. a week had to be paid for – there were some free or assisted places. 'The work is laborious,' said the Union 'and only women physically strong, and with a taste for outdoor work, are fitted for it.'

Land Army recruitment was at first the responsibility of the National Service Ministry but was later taken over by the Ministry of Labour jointly with the Food Production Department. Lloyd George emphasised that, since it was most important that the new Land Army should create a good impression in the early days to counteract the general hostility and distrust of the farming community, the first recruits should be most carefully selected; out of 47,000 only 7,000 were accepted, most of the rejects being medically unfit.

But even when all these sources had been tapped, Lloyd George admitted that there was nothing like enough manual labour to carry through a big increase in cultivation by traditional farming methods – or, he said, even to maintain cultivation at its previous level. One answer would have to be increased mechanisation, but the government did not have the tractors available and anyway some farmers were unwilling to use them. Efforts were made to produce American Fordson tractors at factories in England and at Cork in Ireland under licence from Henry Ford. By the end of the war about 3,000 tractors had been assembled at a Manchester factory from parts supplied by Ford, and about the same number were imported from the factory at Detroit. Another 3,000 of various other makes made a total of some 10,000 by the end of 1918. These early tractors gave inexperienced drivers a good deal of trouble, and a number were killed driving the Fordson. This failed to deter the women of the Corps or the Land Army, many of whom learned to drive tractors.

Lloyd George claimed that in preparations for the 1918 harvest, tractor ploughing accounted for the equivalent of 60,000 acres out of a total of some millions. Of course, other mechanical aids to tillage, aimed at saving labour, were also used, giving what Lloyd George claimed was a permanent fillip to the standard of British farming through mechanisation. Far more land, he said, was put under plough in 1918 than

'Women's Work in Time of War' (early 1916).

in pre-war years, and the yield (mainly through three-fold increase in fertiliser use) was 'considerably higher'.

The work of the Food Production Department soon began to be seen to be effective. It set targets for each county which were given to the WACs while urging them to try and reach their quotas by agreement rather than by compulsion. Before the 1917 harvest, sub-committees were in place at county level with officers and clerks to deal with the administration involved. One of their responsibilities was to assess the labour shortage and decide how to fill vacancies from the Women's Land Army and elsewhere. The Prime Minister, at the centre, soon learnt that things were not well in the shires – or, at least, performance was very uneven. For example, in October 1917 he was told that, of the 21,500 ploughmen that the army had undertaken to supply, only 13,000 had been forthcoming, few of them really skilled. Only 2,500 knew how to plough. The army was, naturally, giving priority to Passchendaele rather than to ploughing.

'The military chiefs scoffed at the idea that the final issue was being fought in Britain's fields and on the high seas,' complained the Prime Minister. 'Every young man snatched for the land was to them a lost recruit.' The result was that a search had to be made in unlikely places to find skilled men. From the London Metropolitan Police Force alone they got 120 skilled ploughmen. Some 4,500 German prisoners were put on to land drainage. Then, of course, there were the women, some of whom proved capable with the plough. Finally, when the Passchendaele offensive was over, the army was persuaded to send back 1,500 ploughmen from the ranks for a three months' stint on the land.

In March 1918, the Germans launched their long-expected offensive and broke through; Lloyd George's critics put this down to a lack of defending troops – though in fact the army commanders had plenty of men whom they had decided to put in the wrong place. But the premier had to give in and find 30,000 men, mainly from agriculture, to send over to France. Happily, more women were now registering, and preparations for the 1918 harvest were well ahead. One important factor was the fact that the real value of the Family Allowances paid to soldiers was falling. In January 1917, the war cabinet resolved that this should stay low so as not to discourage women from taking up war work, particularly on the land.

Compulsory returns from each individual farmer, shown to Lloyd George by Sir Arthur Lee, the new Director General of the Food Production Department, indicated that the winter wheat acreage was at a record 45 per cent over the previous year, or taking both spring and winter wheat, 31 per cent up. By the following month, April, Lee claimed the total acreage (corn and potatoes) to be the highest since 1882 and 2.1 million acres above the 1916 level. He also claimed that this was achieved mainly with a male labour force – taking into account army prisoners of war and volunteers – 200,000 lower than that employed in 1913/14.

Lloyd George's figures indicated that the wheat crop by 1918 was 65 per cent higher than the pre-war average. 'It would have been greater still,' he said, 'if the weather in the latter part of 1918 had not been so foul.' It rained incessantly, but the Home Defence Force put some 70,000 soldiers plus 30,000 prisoners of war to aid bringing in the harvest. Four fifths of it was rescued 'in the teeth of one of the worst seasons imaginable'.

So much for the macro picture. What of the micro? Mrs Wilkins and her team were still hard at work trying to improve the numbers of trained women workers for the Land Army in the face of continued financial problems.

A proliferation of organisations whose declared object was to place more women on the land resulted in confusion, inevitably. A historian calls some of them individually 'of little value' and of 'little practical utility', and 'ineffective'. They included the National Political League formed in 1911 to 'meet the present crisis of shortage of labour in agricultural districts'. Early supporters included Lady Denman, the Lord Mayor of London and numerous other dignitaries. During the early part of the war, the League founded the National Land Council which was responsible for the 'Brownies'. The League had smart offices at 16 St James's Street, London SW1 and held exhibitions at the house of Lady Denman's cousin Lady Cowdray in 16 Carlton House Terrace. 'We live on a fair and fertile island whose green pastures and hedgerows have charmed tourists from all parts of the world,' begins Sarah Tooley's pamphlet on the work of the NPL. This contrasts with the crisp businesslike tones of Mrs Wilkins' communications. The NPL's grant was terminated by the Board of Agriculture on the grounds of inefficiency. The Women's Legion, having formed an agricultural branch under the influence of the Marchioness of Londonderry, also fell out with the Board;

WAR WORK ON THE LAND~A CALL FOR WOMEN.

OUR ENGLAND IS A GARDEN AND SUCH GARDENS ARE NOT MADE

BY SINGING:— OH HOW BEAUTIFUL   AND   SITTING IN THE SHADE

In the words of Mr Kipling.

Lady Londonderry was persuaded to confine their efforts to fruit-bottling and horticulture and relinquish their grant of £200 per year.

The Corps founded by Louisa Wilkins sent out as few as 500 workers at its peak in 1917, mainly for hop-picking and fruit gathering. There was also a separate venture employing a large number of women for flax picking. The Corps was in receipt of a grant of £500 per annum, and this inevitably attracted criticism. The Secretary of the Board of Agriculture remarked in September 1916: 'It is all very well for, say, the local duchess to be brought into a new movement at its inception, mainly because her name is of value in an advertisement and because her pride is useful to provide the necessary funds, but when the movement has once been started, unless the duchess has the good sense to efface herself as quickly as possible and allow the project to be carried on by the people who are primarily interested in it, nine times out of ten the scheme is bound to fail.'

The evidence suggests that the Corps and its associate, the WFGU (they had moved into the same offices at 50 Upper Baker Street in May 1917, with Mrs Benson as joint secretary), remained in the hands of women who were truly interested in training women for the land. They had seen their niche as training the trainers of a large work-force of what Meriel Talbot described as 'village women'. By 1917 this probably numbered some 210,000. Early that year, the Union was asked by the Board of Agriculture to undertake the organisation of training centres for all recruits drawn from the London area, and thirteen such centres were operating within a few weeks. Despite this, a Board of Trade official complained late in 1917 that 'the country is full of these irresponsible training centres for women and they are doing great mischief'.

Harsh as these official words may seem, it is difficult at this distance to make any particularly optimistic judgement about the Land Army itself, in any objective sense of achievements. Yet the fact remains that very few negative comments can be found – it was popular, both as an 'army' and in terms of its individual recruits. Lloyd George only had kindly words for the land girl:

> Breeched, booted and cropped, she broke with startling effect upon the sleepy traditions of the English Countryside. She was drawn from a wide range of classes of society . . . She brought with her enthusiasm and energy, an alert and unprejudiced mind that stimulated the activity of her fellow workers.

It will be noted that, with his sharp eye for a pretty woman, the Welsh Wizard's attention was caught by the appearance and the uniform.

There is some significance in this choice of uniform for the Land Army. It is said that breeches were 'unacceptable in most parts of the country' though they had been worn in Norfolk from the earliest days of the war. The Hon. Lady Fellowes, speaking to a Norwich Women's War Agricultural Committee meeting in July 1917, said that although their clothing included breeches there was 'nothing in the outfit to which the most particular person could take exception. It is a very pretty costume'. And Anne Farewell-Jones recalled that one of her colleagues on the land had such well-cut breeches that the owner of the estate remarked, 'I wish you'd give the name of your tailor to the others'. It is noteworthy, too, that when Harrods and other smart shops took to stocking a kind of uniform it, too, included breeches. An alternative might have been the bloomer, named after the American Mrs Amelia Bloomer, but these had been barred as early as 1898 when the Royal Botanic Garden at Kew (which had recruited a few women students) dropped them in favour of breeches. It is worth asking if the Land Army would have been a name to conjure with after all these years if careful attention had not been given to their form of dress.

The WACs, and the district sub-committees, had an 'outfit officer' responsible for distributing the clothes, because individual items were sometimes in short supply. Of course uniforms of a kind had been available to the Corps and others working on the land prior to the formation of the Land Army, though these were not supplied free of charge as they were to the WLA. Ladies who had not been satisfied with a mere armband awarded after their thirty days' qualifying service could purchase a Harrods Farm Outfit in 'good Genoa Corduroy, excellently cut jacket, button pockets, with convertible storm collar. The britches button at the side, with a buckle and strap at the waist. In dark brown only. All for thirty-five shillings and ninepence. Boots extra at thirty-seven and six.' At this distance of time the uniforms supplied by Harrods and similar outfitters sound more utilitarian than glamorous. But they were superior to the armbands, bottle green baize with an embroidered crown on them, which were presented by the Board of Trade together with a certificate stating: 'Every woman who helps in agriculture during the war is as truly serving her country as the man who is fighting in the trenches, on the sea, or in the air.'

These certificates, and armbands, had been issued from February 1916, when the Board of Agriculture urged the formation in every county of the Women's Farm Labour committees, which were to work with the WACs. Within six months there were sixty-three such county committees, 1,060 district representatives and 4,000 village registrars. As a result, many women registered, either by personally visiting their council offices, or by responding to a call at the door. There was, however, no great enthusiasm for the certificate or the armband, worn by a total of 72,000 women during the spring and summer of 1916. By the year's end their numbers had dwindled to some 60,000 women. Could this be because the whole operation was somewhat drab and utilitarian? Even a scheme to supply clothing through the Co-op stores failed, no doubt because neither the clothing (including a drabbett coat and skirt at 15s.) nor the Co-operative Society had much sex appeal. The same could not be said for the Land Army, which made it clear that those who wore their uniform were members of an army, 'paid soldiers pay, billeted like soldiers and uniformed like soldiers'.

Before the foundation of the Land Army, it had been easy for farmers to make women workers the butt for their scepticism. The *Punch* cartoon (p61) of early 1917 illustrates the farming community's attitude, although during the food crisis of 1916 that community had become more realistic about the role of women, as can be seen from the provincial newspapers around the country. The establishment of the Women's Land Army accelerated the change in the farmers' perceptions.

This was reflected in greater efforts to offer an attractive uniform. Now, a recruit, measured for her outfit before going to the training centre or farm, was fitted up with two overalls, a hat, pair of breeches, boots, pair of leggings, a jersey, a pair of clogs and a mackintosh. Six months later she received a backup of another hat, breeches, boots and leggings. The breeches, though, were the subject of some ribaldry, and, in the early stages, women were ordered never to wear them in public unless they were covered by an overall. Jewellery was also strictly forbidden as it might imply lower moral standards than those acceptable in the agricultural community.

The necessity for high standards of behaviour was stressed in the *Handbook* given to each WLA recruit which pointed out:

> You are doing a man's work and you are dressed rather like a man; but remember that just because you wear a smock and breeches you should take care to behave like an English girl who expects chivalry and respect from everyone she meets. Noisy or ugly behaviour brings discredit, not only upon yourself but upon the uniform, and the whole Women's Land Army. When people see you pass . . . show them that an English girl who is working for her Country on the land is the best sort of girl.

Some thought the girls' uniform an extravagance, like the MP who asked a question on the subject in the House of Commons. He was told that the uniform was absolutely essential if the recruits were to carry out their work efficiently, though the minister admitted that of the quarter of a million pounds spent on the women's branch by the Board of Agriculture in its first fifteen months, over half had gone to expenditure on uniform.

With hindsight it appears that the uniform was as much a matter of morale as of efficiency – after all, village women had managed all these years without a uniform.

The army recruits, however, had to go where they were sent, accept orders from their superiors and submit to a fairly rigorous training period. Initially this lasted only a month, which, Rowland Prothero later admitted, did little except give a rudimentary knowledge of tools and equipment, plus hardening their muscles. Training was later extended to six months, and the girls had to pass a series of tests to determine their efficiency. (It is interesting that they soon became land 'girls' rather than women, just as they were to do in the Second World War.) All kinds of ingenious aids to training were produced – like the two wooden cows on an Essex training farm, fitted with rubber udders, on which the girls would practise milking, followed by a period with nanny goats, before they were allowed to tackle milking valuable dairy cows.

One of the most skilled jobs on the farm, in the days before the tractor, was ploughing with a team. Annie Edwards, who had worked as a maid, but volunteered for farm work near Chichester in Sussex, turned out to be a surprisingly accurate ploughwoman. Her expertise provoked amazement in the men's bar at the village pub, but, she later said, 'one farm hand from a different farm would go back and tell his boss what he had heard at the pub about land girls who ploughed. Two or three farmers would not believe it, and they'd come back on this farm and they'd see me doing it'.

Farmers also had a problem adjusting their views to what was suitable 'woman's work'. In Wales, for example, they tended to regard the land girls as substitute domestic servants. When they asked them to scrub floors, or cook, or nurse the baby they were 'rather perplexed at being met with a blank refusal'. The girls were taunted in the village with 'taking a man's place and driving him into the army'. For the women from upper-middle and upper class homes, the culture was to accept voluntary work, but not to take on a job that was paid. Lady Phyllis MacRae, daughter of the Marquess of Bristol, whose mother had enthusiastically shown her prowess behind the plough, said that in the inter-war years 'it would have been considered very caddish to get a job when there was so much unemployment. You had a home, you had money, you had everything you needed; it would have been wrong to take anyone's job. You were expected to do a lot of voluntary work.' Of course, in the last year or two of the First World War, the respectability of patriotism overcame any such qualms.

For those better-off recruits the standard of accommodation on the farms where they were billeted was often not up to scratch. A Somerset doctor's daughter wrote home to complain that her washing water was rationed to one pint of hot water a day, while her host, the farmer, was the 'dirtiest old man I think I have ever seen in all my life'. His favourite sport was spitting out the bacon rind to the ring of nine cats who sat round the breakfast table. The Times was rather critical of any patronising sentiments, though, and lectured in these terms:

> If you chance to be billeted with a 'village woman', young lady of the Land Army, bear in mind that she is a hostess worth knowing and one who can teach you much.

And, in answer to an appeal, issued by the Army, for more entertainment facilities for the girls, particularly to 'country house parties' and 'tennis club tournaments'. The Times pontificated: 'As for a fuller social life, may not yours and hers be the better and fuller for the sisterhood?' This is in marked contrast to the 1916 poster by the Women's Defence Relief Corps of St John's Wood, one of the many women-on-the-land organisations which failed to get the seal of government approval accorded to the WFGU. They tried to beguile volunteers by offering a 'Free Holiday . . . in the sun Haymaking, Harvesting etc. All who do it are happy and return fitter for having spent a healthy vigorous holiday and with the satisfaction of knowing that they have done their bit.' Sterner times call for sterner tones.

What worried Meriel Talbot was not so much that her girls would be bored by an inadequate supply of house parties, but that 'at any moment some scandal [would] break out and the Department be blamed for inadequate supervision.' She gloomily agreed that the women could not be subjected to strict military discipline, though there were local attempts to produce something of the kind: for example in Leicestershire, where the WAC proposed imposing fines on any who were unruly or absent without leave. In Hertfordshire, an anxious committee also drew up rules for its women recruits:

1. No member is allowed to enter the bar of a public house.
2. Members must be in their billets for the night by 9.30 p.m.
3. Members are not allowed to smoke at work, or in any public place while in uniform.

4. When in uniform, members must always wear the overall in any public place. [This was to hide those provocative breeches.]

5. No communication whatsoever with the German Prisoners of War, whether on or off duty.

Though there is now little evidence to justify the anxieties of Miss Talbot and her team, in 1918 the women's branch appointed eighty full-time welfare officers to visit the workers and check on their morals and their morale as well as to arrange carefully supervised leisure activities such as sewing classes and evening lectures. Another effort to maintain their morale was the establishment in January 1918 of the *Landswoman*, which was a free magazine circulated to all members of the WLA.

The principal barrier to team spirit – indeed any spirit at all – was undoubtedly the harsh nature of life on the land before mechanisation. Long hours hoeing crops, lifting potatoes or root vegetables, weeding and so on, were incredibly monotonous for most. Two girls who worked on a Devon farm recalled their aching backs and arms as they spent whole days 'shaking out heavy manure on the fields'. Another middle class girl billeted on a farm near Godalming in Surrey noted how 'the oats were nearly weeded at last and everybody's hopes are rising of a new job. The thistles have been like a young forest. Peggy did her best to cheer things along by reciting to us as we hoed.' Despite the general drudgery of the work and the frequent bad weather, farmers came round to admiring the girls for the way they stuck to the job. Northamptonshire farmers described them as 'always very keen and very patriotic'.

Some girls went further, performing acts of individual heroism, such as saving a fellow worker from being gored by a bull. Acts like this were recognised by a Distinguished Service Bar (introduced in October 1918) which was attached to the Land Army badge awarded to all members who completed a satisfactory two months' service. In all, between March 1917 and October 1919, there were some 23,000 Land Army girls working on farms, 15,000 of whom had received some sort of training. Of the 12,757 women whose records were maintained, 5,734 worked as milkmaids, 293 as tractor drivers, 3,971 as general field workers, 635 as carters, 260 as ploughwomen and 21 as shepherdesses. Some 84 had specialist training as thatchers. This leaves over 1,500 with no specific activity recorded.

In the book which Rowland Prothero wrote after the war, he described how the growing numbers of women, and their increasing expertise, changed the attitude of farmers. At first, at any meetings attended by agriculturalists, any mention of women was received 'in silence or with disapproving grunts. Three months later there were interjections for or against their employment. Then came an interval when the subject was received with applause, more or less slight . . . The final stage was reached when the real gratitude of the farmers was expressed in the call "Three cheers for the women". The Land Army and the village women had won. So had Mrs Wilkins and Mrs Grosvenor and those members of the Women's Farm and Garden Union who had insisted on a proper training programme for the new workforce which played its part in the feeding of a nation.

In celebration of a Royal Silver Wedding in 1918 the Land Army women march through London in new uniform.

Chapter Seven

Drummed out of the Army

THE OPPORTUNITIES FOR better education and training for women, though they improved considerably after the end of the 1914-18 war, still left vast room for improvement. To some extent this was a hangover from Victorian and Edwardian attitudes when, for example, the British Medical Association had opined that 'continuous mental effort is a danger to young women'. Too much brainwork during puberty, they declared, would damage a woman's future reproductive system. The position was particularly acute in science-based studies. A recent history of

'Harvest Home' featuring the Land Army to the forefront.

HARVEST HOME, 1918.
WITH MR. PUNCH'S JOYOUS CONGRATULATIONS TO THE MINISTER OF AGRICULTURE.

The Women's Farm and Garden Association. :: 29, Park Road, N.W.1.

Land Outfit Department

A good selection of well-cut Coats, Breeches, Overalls, Boots and Leggings are kept in stock and Outfits can be made to measure.

Chester Corduroy Coat ..	£1	11	6	Leggings (Tan and Black)	0	15	6
,, Drill ,, ..	0	12	6	Rubber Wellingtons—			
,, Gaberdine ,, ..	1	7	6	Black	0	15	6
,, Proofed Cantoon	1	5	0	Brown	0	16	6
				Stout Black ditto ..	1	7	6
Breeches—Corduroy ..	0	18	6	Blazers for Members of			
,, Bedford Cord	0	18	6	Association, made to			
,, Gaberdine ..	0	18	6	own measurements			
,, Cantoon ..	0	18	6	£1 0 0 to £1 12 6			
High Field Boots				Members' Ties			
(Tan only)	1	10	0	in W.F.G.A. Colours—			
Short Boots (Tan).. ..	1	0	0	Silk	0	2	11
Ladies' Golfing Boots				Knitted	0	2	3
£1 0 0 to 1 15 0				Mackintoshes from ..	1	1	0
				Hats	0	7	0
Brogue Shoes (Tan) ..	1	5	0	Milkers' Coats	0	12	6
Brogue Shoes (Tan) with				, ,, (Long) ..	0	14	0
Crepe Rubber Soles ..	1	5	0	Stockings—all prices.			

FANCY SMOCKS AND OVERALLS, GARDENING GLOVES, APRONS, TIES, etc., etc., etc.

SEND FOR PRICE LIST.

TERMS CASH.—All goods must be paid for at time of purchase. Goods sent on approval if cost of one or more articles is deposited. 1s. must be enclosed for postage. 5% Discount to members on all purchases over £1.

Small extra charge on all garments made to special measurement

The Association had an outfit department for many years, supplying 'fancy smocks' etc. which were difficult for women to obtain elsewhere.

Benenden, a leading girls' boarding school, relates that as late as 1927 one sixth form girl went up to Oxford for a science degree, having learned what passed for chemistry at a school whose laboratories were not fitted with a gas supply. As she had therefore never been able to see a Bunsen burner, she was obliged to have private tuition before proceeding to university.

The Women's Farm and Garden Association (Incorporated)

(Founded 1899)

President : H.R.H. THE PRINCESS LOUISE, DUCHESS OF ARGYLL

OBJECTS.

1. **To unite all professional women workers in Agriculture, Horticulture, and** allied subjects, and those interested in such work for women into a strong Central Association.

2. **To help and advise women in all matters connected with these professions.**

3. **To further the interests of women by seeking their due representation on** public bodies concerned with matters relating to Agriculture and Horticulture.

4. **To watch events and to make representation to public bodies on matters** relating to Agriculture and Horticulture, especially with regard to those affecting the interests of women.

ADVANTAGES TO BE GAINED BY JOINING THE ASSOCIATION.

1. **PROFESSIONAL TRAINING :** The Association gives information as to training in existing institutions in the various branches of Agriculture and Horticulture.

2. **EMPLOYMENT:** The Association keeps a register of trained workers who have specialised in various branches of Agriculture and Horticulture, and endeavours to obtain suitable appointments.

3. **EMIGRATION:** The Association is in touch with the Society for the Oversea Settlement of British Women, and has the latest information with regard to openings for women landworkers in all the Dominions.

4. **JOURNAL: Members receive a free copy of the Annual Report and Journal,** also copies of the Quarterly Leaflets. This is a valuable medium for disseminating information; for bringing persons interested in Agriculture and Horticulture in touch with one another; for advertising produce; for arranging partnerships, etc., etc.

5. **CLUB HOUSE: A Hostel run on Club lines, which contains a dining-room,** bedrooms, comfortable reading and sitting rooms, running h. & c. water in all rooms. Members of the W.F. & G.A. can join at an additional subscription of 10s. per annum. Unfurnished rooms for permanent residents.

6. **PRODUCE : Arrangement for exhibition and sale of Members' farm and** garden produce on the Association's stands at Agricultural and Horticultural shows.

7. **LAND OUTFIT DEPARTMENT: The Association has a Department for well-cut** Overalls, Breeches, Mackintoshes, Boots, etc. Discount is allowed to members.

8. **LENDING LIBRARY of Farm and Garden books.**

TERMS OF MEMBERSHIP.

Subscription to Association.

Class A.	As a Life Member.	One payment of £10	**Additional**
Class B.	As an Associate Member.	21/- per annum	**Subscription to**
Class C.	As an Ordinary Member. (those who are working on their own land)	12/6 per annum	**Club House**
Class D.	As a Working Member. (those who are working for a salary).	7/6 per annum	**10/- per annum**
Class E.	(for the use only of past and present students of Colleges affiliated to the W.F. & G.A.)	5/- per annum	for members joining under Class A, B, C, D, and E.
Class F.	Combined Subscription for Permanent Residence in Club House.	31/- per annum	

FOR ALL FURTHER PARTICULARS APPLY:

THE SECRETARY, COURTAULD HOUSE, BYNG PLACE, TORRINGTON SQUARE, LONDON, W.C.I.

TELEPHONE: MUSEUM 1281.

The pioneer founders of the WFGU had largely been ladies who believed they were doing good for their sex by putting them in the way of training for work in agriculture or horticulture. Those that followed had a different motivation, but the change towards acceptance of women as part of the natural rural workforce did not come about quickly. One of the symptoms of change, or rather the lack of it, was the economic environment.

For example one of the WFGA members described the years 1930 to 1932 as terrible times when women trying to make their way on the farm were dogged by a widespread feeling of insecurity. 'So much unemployment and misery existed. Even if one was lucky enough to have found a job, one worked terribly hard to keep it. And to ask for an increase in pay was unheard of and tantamount to risking dismissal.'

Wages were still appalling. Dr Kate Barrett recalled that when she started work in 1902 payments for a farm worker were a mere 5d. an hour (equivalent to 70p today). By the 1930s they were 30s. a week (£39 today). For a woman to receive a wage of this kind she needed some sort of qualification. In 1900 there had been only a handful of places where she could obtain one – now, in the inter-war years, there were more, though some were restricted. A girl leaving grammar or public school was ineligible for the one-year training courses set up by local councils, which were only open to sons and daughters of farmers and farm workers (in practice, many local councils could not afford the separate accommodation obligatory for women students in pre-pill days).

However as well as the three main women's colleges – Swanley, Studley and Waterperry – a number of private farm and garden schools and pupilships catered for those women who could afford the fees. These colleges and schools had to manage despite, in most cases, no government or council grants. Several offered degrees – Reading, Studley and Oxford for example. Inevitably the cost was prohibitive for the majority and the intake was from middle class families. By 1939 college fees were around £120 per annum including board and lodging as well as tuition. (A small family car, at this time, cost £100-£120 and the courses lasted two or three years. A semi-skilled labourer's wage was £3 per week.)

Most women wanting to branch out into farming or horticulture were keen to join the WFGA because its employment bureau could help them find posts once they had

Miss Antoinette Vanderpant (standing) with Chairman Lady Victoria Hicks Beach at the 1939 AGM.

their diploma or degree. The best-educated women got the best jobs – but even those less favoured found that education was an essential key to success.

Three prominent members of the Association have left testaments to its role in the 1920s and 1930s. The first of these is Miss Antoinette Vanderpant. Trained as a historian, she had found herself working with Dr Kate Barrett (see below) at the outset of the First World War. The two women were running a flax pullers' camp on Salisbury Plain which grew so quickly that it was soon taken over by the Women's National Land Service Corps.

To many of its members, Miss Vanderpant *was* the WFGA from 1917 onwards. Though physically she was a very spare figure she had a tough sort of attitude and was determined that the members should get justice, find suitable jobs and so on. At the same time she was practical and would without hesitation give a lecture on the importance of wearing the right sort of boots. In fact council members in the main failed to appreciate her true worth. It has been said that they 'treated her as if she were a superior parlour maid'. She wrote the following account at the end of the Second World War:

From 1917 I can speak personally, as I joined the Land Service staff in the summer of that year. The government continued to recognise the Corps as the authorised voluntary organisation for placing women on the land and also made it their agent for recruiting and placing all seasonal workers. The WFGU was also asked to undertake the organisation of training centres for Land Army recruits in the London area; over 9,000 women had already been sent out by the Corps.

In 1918 the Corps had to supply 2,000 recruits for the flax harvest and the Corps was only 8,450 strong. That was also the year in which the late Lady Lionel Phillips said that a club was needed for the girls to use as they passed through London. Our offices were on the present site of the Abbey Road Building Society offices, opposite Baker Street station, and there was an empty house next door. Lady Phillips took this and furnished it at her own expense, and it was a boon!

When demobilisation came in 1919 the government grants came to an end, and the war-time workers gave up, although many women did continue to pass into the colleges for regular training. Then came the eternal money question; how to carry on? The WFGU and the WNLSC were combined and started post-war activities as the Women's Farm and Garden Association. There were three things to tackle: to build up a permanent membership, to make some money, and to do some reconstructive work. We were very poor and the staff were cut to myself and a typist, plus a part-time worker. Through a bank and other loans three nearby houses were taken in Park Road, opposite Clarence Gate, Regent's Park, and a new club started which took Bedford College students as well as our own members.

In three years we had turned the corner. The Warden Miss Dunnell organised the club so well that she was able to pay off all the loans.

Small Holding Colony was also established near Lingfield in Surrey in 1920 financed by Miss Courtauld and Mrs Wilkins. Through their generous help over 98 acres were purchased and divided into smallholdings with cottages which were let to women at an economic rent. Some tenants, having graduated, moved to larger acreages and their holdings were re-let, others bought their land until by 1932 only one tenanted holding was left and the scheme was brought to an end. Although not easy to run it was considered to have been a successful co-operative venture.

As the 1920s went on we began to grow: we had stands at shows, Chelsea, the Royal Agricultural Show, and a big effort with members' produce at the London Dairy Show. Our publications were better: we produced an Annual Report and Journal, plus quarterly Leaflets. The brightest spots of these build up years were, to my mind, the incorporation of the Association under the Companies Act of 1929, and the affiliation of the horticultural colleges in the same year.

The lease of the Park Road houses was running out and we had to look for new premises where we could have a bigger club, as undoubtedly this was the means of bringing in an income with which to increase the Association's activities. This came through the generosity of Miss K. M. Courtauld, and we moved into our own free-hold, Courtauld House, near Gower Street, in 1932; it was a strange coincidence that the Association was formed in a house in Gower Street in 1899.

Now indeed all seemed set fair. The new house was soon full, and the cost of domestic wages and upkeep not what it is today. There were forty beds, a library and spacious public rooms. The time had come when we could see clearly that in order to decentralise the work and increase the membership there should be some foundation of County Groups in order that members could meet and get to know each other, discuss matters of interest and importance in their work, so that where necessary action could be taken. Members were all in favour, and on a small scale the County Group Scheme, as we called it, began to take shape.

Then came 1938 and Munich, and with it the dashing of all our hopes. Instead of developing County Groups, in that one year before the war, we had to organise a holiday scheme so that interested women could learn a little about farm and garden work. We transferred all the women who had done this holiday work to the second Women's Land Army in 1939. The story of the Association during the Second World War, and the hard knocks it had taken are, briefly, as follows: the evacuation of London University in 1939 reduced the number of residents in the club and few of our own members came to stay in there because of the air raids. There were, however, a handful of people still living at the club from 1939 until Courtauld House suffered severe air raid damage in September 1940. The house then had to be closed and the office staff removed for three months until first-aid repairs could be done.

The offices reopened on 1st January 1941, and carried on for the rest of the war. The residential side was taken over by a war organisation, and it was not possible for us to regain possession of the club until August 1945. The damage done to the house and furniture took over a year to make good, but a few students and members were accommodated. It was at this time (1945) when the war damage repairs were being completed that dry rot was discovered, and one exterior wall of the house had to be almost entirely rebuilt. This took over two years at a cost of approximately £7,000. No war damage claim covered this, and the WFGA found itself burdened with serious debt. But for this, with the club once more in commission, we should have been self-supporting. It was a cruel blow, after we had come through so much during the war, and had escaped any further damage. The two years of rebuilding were an ordeal and it was not until 1946 that all rooms could be used. Nevertheless during those war years a great deal was achieved and I should like to mention in particular the efforts made in early 1940, with the support of other organisations, to obtain a National Agricultural Minimum rate of pay for women workers, and the establishment of the Garden Apprenticeship Scheme in the same year.

Miss Katherine Courtauld at the farm in Essex which
she managed on a commercial basis.

MISS KATHERINE COURTAULD

Katherine Courtauld was born on 13 July 1856, a member of the wealthy and radical family which had factories and farms in Essex and other parts of the country. The Courtaulds were Calvinist Huguenots who arrived in England from France about 1685 to escape religious persecution. Starting as silversmiths, in 1687 they switched to silk weaving in the Essex area. Finally, by exploiting the invention of rayon, they built a textile empire and by the mid-nineteenth century they had made their fortune.

Miss Courtauld's immediate family was, in some ways, typical of the Victorian radical establishment. Her father became Liberal MP for Maldon (Essex) then crossed the floor to join the Tories, an unusual route. Her great grandfather had travelled in a different – if equally unconventional – way, going many times to America, where he attempted to inspire the socialist Robert Owen. We know nothing about Miss Courtauld's education (presumably under a governess) but it may, too, have been unusual, like her half sister's whose determination to become a doctor could not be balked by the fact that no university in the UK would take her – so she took a degree at Brussels, later serving as a medic on the battlefields of the First World War. In 1878 when Miss Courtauld was twenty one, her father, who lived in Gosfield, Essex, bought Knights Farm in nearby Colne Engaine which he gave to his daughter – at the time an unusually, perhaps uniquely generous and enlightened gesture, even for a rich man. At first she personally farmed 243 acres, later increasing this to 2,000 acres.

Before attempting farming on her own account, Miss Courtauld had assisted for some years in the management of another farm owned by her father, though even then she lamented the fact that there were no agricultural schools for women.

An article in *The Ladies Field* of October 1899, which describes her as a 'Fair Farmeress', says that at that date she bought all her own stock, attending the sales and 'bidding just as the other farmers do'. Her staff of fifteen men and boys 'all work admirably under the farmer's direction'.

By 1899, she possessed a herd of ten Jerseys and some black Galloways, a flock of some eighty registered Suffolk sheep and about a hundred pigs. 'Poultry is another important consideration' with a 'feathered flock for table use'. However the orchard, which surrounded the house, was Miss Courtauld's primary concern. In later life she was to achieve national fame as a fruit grower. Her interest in farm education was illustrated by her having taken in several pupils at Knights Farm. She was also a supporter of the smallholdings movement pioneered by Louisa Wilkins. In 1920 she and Wilkins set up a 98-acre farm at Lingfield, Surrey for training women.

Miss Courtauld probably attended the meeting in London which led to the formation of the WFGU and, though there is no record that she was or was not one of the small band of stalwarts who formed the original committee, she soon appears in the records as having been elected a member in late 1900.

Miss Courtauld never married. Sometime before she moved into Knights Farm, she had acquired a companion, Miss Mary Gladstone, known as Aunt Mary to the family. She was a close relative of the Prime Minister. The Gladstones, who lived nearby, were also relatives by marriage of Lady Grosvenor and Meriel Talbot.

The two women were more than passably good looking and led an active social life. Both were keen sportswomen. Miss Courtauld rode side saddle all her hunting life with the East Essex Hunt and with her companion would travel about the county in their one-horse trap. Miss Courtauld was also a fine shot and her diaries are full of references to substantial kills of game on the estate. Such hunting, shooting and fishing activities were somewhat unusual for a woman in Victorian and Edwardian days, but the most unusual of all was Miss Courtauld's enthusiasm for another family pursuit, sailing. She owned a yacht, the *Petrona*, and again her diaries are full of references to sailing, racing and visits to yachting clubs. Later, it is not clear exactly when, she adopted a more masculine stance, which suited her strong and forceful personality. Her hair was now cut in an Eton crop. Although she always wore a skirt in preference to trousers, the upper part of her body was encased in mannish waistcoats and jackets, a stiff white collar and tie at her neck, and on her head at appropriate times a pork pie hat. After her death (at Knights Farm on 5 July 1935) a portrait of her, still in the family's possession, was sent for valuation to Christie's who made the pardonable mistake of listing it in the catalogue as 'Portrait of Gentleman with Dog'. She made a permanent contribution to the WFGA by giving it the freehold of a house in London which was for many years its headquarters.

Portrait of Gentleman with Dog.

A similar account of the position of women over the inter-war period was given by Dr Kate Barrett, Miss Vanderpant's friend, at the 1959 AGM of the Association, though her emphasis is on the economic changes that had taken place. She was one of the earliest students at Swanley and its principal from 1919 for twenty-three years. She wrote:

In the 1914-18 war great stress was laid on the need to grow food, wool and flax. Subsidies were available for educational agriculture and a stimulus was given to the employment of women. The Land Army was formed. After the war the subsidies were dropped, but money was found for scholarships for some wives and daughters of agricultural workers. Many women had good opportunities. Farm Institutes were established and the subject of Rural Domestic Science recognised, also providing posts for women. During that war many members of our Association went harvesting during the summer vacation; corn, flax, raspberries, and other crops. In Scotland we were paid one farthing per pound for picking raspberries for Tommy's (the soldiers') jam – the rate for the job. Quick pickers could earn enough to pay for their food, harvesting 90lb in three three-hour shifts. But the slower ones had to supplement their earnings.

By 1939 the statutory wage for the agricultural labourer had risen considerably but it was still only 35s. per week for a man and about 25s. for a woman. The basic wage now [1959] is 160s. and 121s. 6d. respectively for a forty-six hour week. The average salary of the trained practical worker in 1939 was about 25s. per week with board and residence or £2 10s. to £3 without. It was difficult to live on these sums, but the most serious drawback was the lack of advancement, always the trouble in the agricultural industry. The present rate of pay for trained workers is rather more than the basic rate for labourers. There is no graded scale and some will remember the effort made by this Association to interest the National Farmers' Union in such a scheme for both men and women, but nothing much has been done.

A third account is given by Lady Hicks Beach, a stalwart of the WFGA and council member since 1927.

My first experience of the WFGA was when my sister and I got into touch with Miss Vanderpant and the employment bureau over the staffing of a farm at Coln St Aldwyn in Gloucestershire which we took over after the 1914-18 war. For some time we had only women working on it, but though we continued always with a forewoman we gradually replaced the other women by the men from our parish who came back from the army. Later, about 1927, I was invited to become a member of the WFGA Council and I found its meeting very interesting. Naturally I remember some of the happenings while I served on it and some personalities more than others. Miss Courtauld was an outstanding person – plainly a really fine woman, even on slight acquaintance. Miss MacQueen was another whom I soon learnt to admire both for her character and for her ability; she was widely experienced and, besides a sense of humour, had the qualities of wisdom and cool judgement which are so valuable. Mrs Cross also had that combination of qualities, and added to them the power of almost legal analysis which I can only suppose she inherited, or learnt, from her distinguished father. She and I became firm friends, and I know that we of the WFGA owe much to her steadfast work all through the difficult war years.

On the financial side we were fortunate in our advisors. Miss Egerton, many years our treasurer, was wont to laugh down her own share in those matters but she was both shrewd and co-operative. Miss Dunnell, secretary of the club and also (I think) for some time co-treasurer with Miss Egerton, surprised and impressed me with her financial knowledge. Miss Ekins was another helpful and practical member; so was Miss Jean Mason (the dairy expert and close friend of Miss Courtauld), a charming and wide-minded person. Dr Kate Barrett brought her great ability to the Council, informing with her zeal for the cause of women in agriculture and her vivid interest in the progress of agricultural education. Among the other women I knew I must also testify to the many years of devoted work by Miss Russell as manageress of the club, whose members received such a wide sympathy from her. Nor can I leave out Mrs Norman Grosvenor, under whom I served most happily for some years. The Luxmoore Committee had been set up in 1941, so we appointed a small sub-committee of our own to consider the position and the needs of women in particular, and in 1942 it produced a memorandum which was printed and sent to the Luxmoore Committee. We had very few meetings, but the five busy people serving with me on the committee were very helpful with their special knowledge of different aspects of the matter.

Courtauld House, donated to the Association by Miss Courtauld and the mainstay of its finances for many years.

The move to Courtauld House, donated by Miss Courtauld as headquarters and club in early 1933, had changed the character of the WFGA because it cemented the 'club' nature of the organisation for many of its ordinary members. There is talk of members 'wanting to get to know each other', and these were ordinary women who could take advantage of the rooms at 5s. a night including a 'plain' breakfast. In practice, very few working members stayed at the clubhouse except during Chelsea, or Dairy Show weeks. The main part of the accommodation income was dependent on non-members – many of them post-graduate students of the university and similar. Finally there were some rooms for permanent residents who paid only £1 or £2 per night for this pleasant little *pied à terre* in central London. There was hot and cold water in all rooms, described as 'running water' because it was not brought to the rooms by hand-carried jugs as was the common practice in hotels at that time.

Advertising from World War II *(Imperial War Museum).*

These pleasant facilities resulted in increased membership. For example in 1934 alone there were another 152 members of whom about a third joined through affiliated groups at horticultural colleges like Swanley. Total membership at this time was some 1,250. Nevertheless the Thirties were bad years for employment; many women could not pay their subscription and so had to resign from membership. What is more, the WFGA believed that a 'number of women professionally engaged in outdoor work' were not yet members – despite their firm belief that 'all women agricultural and horticultural workers should belong to a central society which exists to work in their interests'.

Another aspect of WFGA activities in the inter-war period was the interest in what was known as garden design but came to be known as landscape architecture or garden architecture. A course had been started by Miss Agar, a member of the WFGA committee since 1907, at Swanley Horticultural College, but she attracted a mere dozen or so pupils of whom only about three took up work in this new profession – Mary Tyler (née Milner) Maisie Cunningham and, most significantly, Brenda Colvin.

The three women added distinction to the women's garden movement, despite pursuing careers somewhat at variance with the main thrust of the Association's work – indeed it is probably true to say that the WFGA had little to do with garden design, that arm of the gardening profession which currently attracts so many educated women. It is interesting to speculate whether, under the influence of these distinguished horticulturists, the twin disciplines of practical gardening and landscape design could not have come closer together, even joined forces. In fact the two have largely remained separately thought of, separately taught and separately practised to the present day.

MISS M. AGAR

Miss Madeline Agar, an American by birth, was one of the early members whose interest was in horticulture rather than in advancing the feminist cause. A pupil at Swanley College in the mid-1890s she began her professional career at Wycombe Abbey School for girls where Miss Dove employed her to teach as well as garden. In 1906 she succeeded Miss Wilkinson as landscape gardener to the Metropolitan Public Gardens Association. A member of the WFGA committee from 1907, she was in fact the Association's oldest member, having joined in 1900 at the request of Mrs Chamberlain, in whose flower shop the early meetings were held. Later she became treasurer. She was a founder member of the Landscape Architect Institute and her contacts with American architects and landscape engineers in the early days of this century had a great influence on her pupils. In addition to her design work on private gardens and larger scale projects like Wimbledon Common she wrote several books including *Garden Design in Theory and Practice* (1902) and the *Book of Gardening for the Sub-Tropics* (1922) which included a glossary of Arabic gardening terms. She died, aged ninety-seven, in 1967.

Eventually Colvin herself set up a private practice and, in due course, the small group organised their own professional association. Brenda Colvin continued to support the WFGA until her death in 1981 and indeed was one of the dynamic group of members who helped to set the Association on its feet again after the trauma of the outbreak of war. Another student of distinction, Sylvia Crowe (who died in 1998), also achieved fame as a designer: she was a pupil of Colvin and a lifelong member of the WFGA though she did not take such an active part in it as Brenda Colvin had. Both Colvin and Crowe were created DBE for their contributions to landscape design,

The outbreak of the Second World War in 1939 will almost certainly come to be seen as a watershed year by future historians, much as we consider 1066 now. Many changes in attitudes had occurred during the First World War, but it was nothing to the torrent of change that occurred, almost overnight, with the outbreak of the Second World War, and swept away all the old attitudes, values and preconceptions of the Victorian and Edwardian worlds. For elderly upper class women reared in the 1870/80s it was a cataclysmic event – like the dinosaurs, they hadn't seen it coming and couldn't adapt. In the late Thirties the WFGA Council still comprised many of these women, who had joined it in its early years, thirty or forty years before. No doubt their opinions would carry considerable weight because of their long connection and support for the Association, but they were too old – tired and lacking in energy, no doubt – to recognise and adapt to the new challenges posed by an imminent war. After the Munich crisis of September 1938 a Holiday Land Service Scheme was hurriedly organised so that women could gain a little experience of farm and garden work. However the Council publicly expressed the opinion, in its minutes and in the Annual Report, that its work remained 'primarily concerned with trained and experienced women and their main endeavour must be to uphold their interests during a time then they may be seriously affected by an influx of temporary volunteers'.

One younger member of the Council who disagreed with this attitude was Lady Denman. She had turned her energies in the inter-war years to both the Family Planning Association (which gave her a taste for fighting the Establishment) and the Women's Institute, of which she was a very active and long serving chairman. She foresaw the need for a re-formed WLA and set up Women's Committees in every county. On 28th August 1939, a mere five days before the outbreak of war, she let her own mansion at Balcombe Place become the headquarters of the Women's Land Army. She chose her staff from among her friends at the Women's Institute and the Family Planning Association; her two closest aides were Inez Jenkins of the Institute and Margaret Pike of the FPA. Thus it was that when Robert Hudson took over from Mr Dorman-Smith at the Ministry of Agriculture he found an already established Women's Land Army structure that relied little on the WFGA.

"Now, Miss Fforbes-Wattson, have you had any experience of agricultural work?"

The Association, with its publicly expressed 'elitist' attitude, had been side-lined and the ill-advised Holiday Land Service Scheme was incorporated into the Women's Land Army. The old order was collapsing and failing to maintain the traditions of the Association, which should have been protesting about some of the poor conditions of service that the WLA volunteers had to face: county committees formed under the auspices of the Women's Institute and the Family Planning Association may have been very suitable for overseeing the moral welfare of the land girls, but had little first-hand appreciation of the practical problems of young women embarking on hard manual labour in an alien environment, or of the poor pay structure and working conditions embodied in the service.

The actual outbreak of war in September 1939 had many immediate practical consequences. Travel was particularly affected: petrol rationing at one gallon per month for a private car resulted in most vehicles being laid up for the duration and an almost total loss of bus and coach services. Train services were still at full strength, theoretically (because they ran on Welsh steam coal not imported oil), but in practice were constantly disrupted and delayed by special movements of troops and military equip-

Irene Gill, former shop assistant from Salford, wheeling farm manure. The reality of farm work was often a long way from expectations.

ment and later by air raids. All these troubles were compounded by the draconian black-out regulations. In London, with the immediate flight from the capital of many government and university offices and departments, in anticipation of aerial bombardment, Courtauld House lost almost all its residents. It could contribute nothing to the Association's funds and the Council of Management virtually collapsed with only a handful of members and the indefatigable Miss Vanderpant keeping the routine activities alive. When London air raids actually commenced in 1940, the clubhouse received severe damage from bomb blast and had to be evacuated for some months while temporary repairs were undertaken. It was the greatest pity that this possibility had not been foreseen. If the opportunity had been taken, at the outbreak of war, to immediately hand Courtauld House over to the government for the duration, for a rental, to accommodate service women and WLA in transit, many of the Association's later troubles would never have arisen. As it was, by 1941 the Association was in a financial crisis such as it had not experienced since the acquisition of Courtauld House.

A committee of investigation and reconstruction was formed under Dr Kate Barrett with Miss Ekins (principal of Studley College since 1922) and Miss Mason as members. Overall the finances of the Association were described as extremely serious. A major reason for this was the forced closure of Courtauld House, with the inevitable loss of rental income for some while. The committee decided that the only thing to do was to let the house for the duration of the war. It was rented to a government organisation which provided hostel accommodation for Londoners who had lost their homes during the blitz. However, the Association was able to retain its offices in the building and store its club furniture there. The employment service of the WFGA was free to find jobs for women who were, themselves, exempt from compulsory call-up regulations, e.g. those over thirty years of age. However, no women were placed in 'private' gardens unless the owners of the garden had a certificate of approval from the local War Agricultural Committee stating that 80 per cent of their working hours should be spent on food production: this excluded any time spent cultivating flowers or so called 'luxury fruits'.

A development from this was the proposal, first mooted in 1940, and finalised in 1941, to give girls a six-month grounding in practical work under a head gardener, the aim being to specialise in food production. The president, Lady Lucas, threw herself wholeheartedly into the scheme, establishing a 'probation centre' in her own home, Woodyates Manor, near Salisbury. Miss Jex-Blake was appointed as organiser of the scheme, with a grant from the Pilgrim Trust. Though most of the County Farm Institutes had been closed for ordinary tuition since the start of the war, the WFGA undertook to see if the counties would make grants to girls for further training. They agreed to do so and in 1941, at Christmas, a leaflet was issued which was to be a significant indicator of the route the Association would follow post-war. This was the Garden Apprenticeship Scheme. During the following winter about a hundred apprentices were in training for a six-month course and there was 'no difficulty' in finding places for them at the end of the period. Grants were available from about

Miss E.R. Ekins, Principal of Studley College from
1922 (second right).

twenty county authorities, on the basis that the trainees had a 'sound training in food production with a view to semi-skilled women replacing men'.

The Association during the post-war years made great efforts to enrol the Ministry of Agriculture in support of continuation of the apprenticeship scheme, since both recognised that this had been a successful initiative. The Ministry agreed a new scheme after 31st March 1946, providing girls with twelve months' tuition instead of six, and with a minimum entry age of seventeen rather than sixteen years. It renewed its grant of £500 towards expenses, and the Pilgrim Trust made a further contribution of a similar sum. A rather miserly 50 guineas was allotted by the Royal Horticultural Society.

It has already been noted that a special committee was set up under Dr Barrett to try and reverse the wartime fall-off in membership. One result of their deliberations was to appoint seventeen Regional Officers to recruit locally. This was effective, and during 1942 there were some 250 new members as against fewer than a hundred in the previous year. The first three months of 1943 saw a further 125 applications. This growth in membership, plus an increase in subscriptions to 10s. (7s. 6d. for those joining from affiliated bodies), was helpful in almost balancing the books. Nevertheless the ability to supply labour continued to be poor. Employers requested 1,237 workers in 1942/3, two-thirds of them for horticultural work, but the employment department had only 117 workers on its books.

Membership continued to rise in 1943/4, when the total reached 1,265, though there was still a shortfall of income and the Association was forced to dip into its slender capital resources. By 1943/44 the Regional Scheme, established by the reconstruction committee, was proving its value. Membership was increasing where it was active, and the scheme was providing the (much overdue) channel for members to put their opinions to Council. In the new national climate of planning for post-war improvements a strong Council was forming of young, hard-working professional women with an understanding of the needs of their working contemporaries which could never have been achieved by the 'old guard' whom they had supplanted.

With the end of the war in 1945, the Association regained control of Courtauld House, only to discover that the whole east wall was affected by dry rot. Rebuilding work was in progress throughout most of 1946, and the Association was lumbered with a capital debt of £7,000, about £91,000 at 1999 prices. This was an appalling blow – only mitigated by the appointment of Miss Gillian Forster as hostel warden: she laboured tirelessly and successfully to keep the clubhouse in constant full occupation, coping cheerfully and capably with all the postwar shortages of equipment, labour and food rationing, and providing a steady income to underpin the administration of the Association

Not only were there these difficulties with the clubhouse, the heart of the WFGA, but the employment bureau, which had been the lynch-pin of the Association for so many years, was in difficulties due to the shortage of labour while the demobilisation of service personnel proceeded at such a slow pace. Jobs were so plentiful that even college leavers could source their own without recourse to the employment service. Out of a demand for well over a thousand women for employment a mere eighty-seven could be placed. Only seventeen farm workers registered with the WFGA for employment in the year 1945/6. There remained strict controls on those employed in gardens and farms; women below sixty years of age working in 'scheduled' establishments were not free to leave their jobs without official permission. This was not readily forthcoming.

In addition to support for women through its employment bureau, the WFGA had naturally continued, through the war years, to support the cause of women farm workers generally. As already noted, it prepared a lengthy memorandum for the Luxmoore Committee on the subject of post-war reconstruction of agricultural and horticultural education, and was also in contact with such bodies as the Central Agricultural Wages Board. The latter, formed in 1942, authorised a weekly minimum wage for women land workers of 45s. for a forty-eight hour week in winter, fifty hours in summer, that is 11d. per hour. Unhappy settlements such as this led to a

Potato planters in the early days of mechanisation in World War II, though most potatoes were still planted by hand.

Memorandum from the Association to the Royal Commission on Equal Pay, as well as studies on such subjects as housing for rural workers and the future for women working in public parks. A minor but significant victory was the breakthrough announcement by the Royal Botanic Gardens, Kew, in 1946, that 'in future women would be equally eligible with men as student gardeners there'.

As always, accident played a part in progress. Dr Barrett's *alma mater* at Swanley had been closed after bombing by the *Luftwaffe* leaving her with time on her hands. Though snapped up in an advisory capacity by Wye College, she was able to devote her great talents, backed by her knowledge and energy, to the requirements of the WFGA. She had been a member since her student days and now she became a driving force behind its reconstruction.

In 1947 Miss Vanderpant retired from her post as organising secretary after thirty years of outstanding service to the Association. The last of the 'old guard' who had worked with her for many years also retired at this time.

As new organising secretary, Miss Barbara Crosland, had been selected – a trained horticulturist herself, but with wide organisational and manipulative skills, very good with people, a good sense of humour, popular with the members and inspiring instant confidence. She and Miss Forster combined to raise the maximum income from Courtauld House and from the membership to tackle the overhanging debt. Miss Forster kept Courtauld House bulging at the seams all the time, with energy, efficiency and a cheerful welcome, and over the next few years they combined with members to set up stands at the many emerging post-war shows such as Chelsea.

Dr Barrett had taken over officially as hon. treasurer after the eventual retirement of Mrs F.J.K. Cross; Lady Nathan had taken over the Presidency from Lady Tweedsmuir and gave great support to the Association for the next twenty years. Her knowledge and contacts were particularly valuable in 1963 when Courtauld House was sold. Miss Jex Blake, a working member who had been running the Garden Apprenticeship Scheme, became chairman and reorganised the old system of standing committees to make a streamlined Council of Management whose members were all involved in, and responsible for, policy, working through *ad hoc* committees as required. Members were elected by postal ballot for a term of three years, and after two terms, had to stand down for a year. This system is still in force and makes for a constant infusion of new blood and ideas on to the Council. The Association at last had a formidably strong team to face the future.

DR KATE BARRETT

Kate Barrett's life was intertwined with that of Swanley College, Kent, from 1902 when she became a student there at the age of eighteen. This establishment had been founded in 1889 as The Horticultural College and Produce Company, a private venture believed to have been the first of its kind anywhere in the world. The first thirteen students paid £80 a year and two years later the first five women students enrolled. The governess and managers of the new college had included what we should now call feminists, and they also included male well-wishers who were per-

Dr Kate Barrett.

suaded of the advantages of a scientific and horticultural training for women. At the top of the list of supporters was Empress Frederick of Prussia, eldest daughter of Queen Victoria and mother of the Kaiser.

As early as 1900 it was decided not to take any more male students (the reasons for this are not fully known, but it may have had something to do with the influence of Professor Richard Tabor who had been a student at the college and joined the staff as a lecturer and tutor in 1898). The girls wore a uniform – a dark smock except for the dairy work when they wore white – which was not redesigned for twenty years. From its early days the college offered a two-year course leading to a diploma (the Royal Horticultural Society's National Diploma was not inaugurated until 1913 but initially it made no test of practical compliance).

Kate Barrett stayed on for a further two years after obtaining the diploma to become a botany demonstrator. She then won a national scholarship at the Royal College of Science at South Kensington (the fourth Swanley student and the second Swanley woman to do so). Here she obtained her BSc with honours in Botany and returned in 1910 to the college to take a place vacated by Richard Tabor. She joined a staff of a nominal fifteen professors and lecturers, plus demonstrators, some of them part-time. By 1912, possibly after pressure from Miss Barrett, the Women's Agricultural and Horticultural Union, of which she was a member, set up a National Diploma in Horticulture to which a number of Swanley students aspired. It is said that the standard was 'extremely high' providing an all-round practical training acquired during a full course of nine terms. Later in 1916, the curriculum changed after London University instituted a BSc Horticulture course. Earlier than this, about the time that Miss Barrett was a student at the college, its board of governors had made its first approaches to secure affiliation with the university, a move which did not achieve final success until another forty years had passed.

Swanley had its own farm, with a few cows and pigs, though the main emphasis was horticultural. There was also an attempt, during Miss Barrett's period there (actually from 1903) to constitute a colonial branch with its own curriculum. Its aim was 'to carry out the valuable indoor and outdoor training for girls going forth to our colonies, who would be qualified to maintain beyond the seas the best traditions of English home life'. It will be recalled that the WAHIU had similar 'international' aspirations. Swanley was more successful, passing some 250 students through the branch until the war caused admissions to dwindle and, in 1916, the doors to close so that horticulture became, once more, the main feature of tuition.

In the year in which Kate Barrett had enrolled as a student, a new principal had been elected. Frances R. Wilkinson was the sister of the acting principal who, like all his predecessors, had been a man. His wife had been, at one time, secretary of the college. Frances Wilkinson had been on the committee of the so-called women's branch of the college (this was now dissolved as it became women only) and like the other Wilkinsons she was not only a dedicated feminist but was well-off and generous with it. Her first years she took no salary, donating her income to the building of a greenhouse. Miss Wilkinson, like Miss Barrett, was an active WAHU member. Both were feminists and were amused when the governing body told a group of students who wished to march in a Women's Suffrage demonstration in London, carrying a banner, that they could have permission to do so only if they walked as women gardeners and did not use the Swanley name.

In 1916 Miss Wilkinson's poor health forced her to retire, though she remained a governor and a WAHU council member. She arranged for Kate Barrett (now on the staff of the Royal College of Science) to head a newly founded group of ex-students, representing a valuable source of potential.

For a major part of the First World War, Miss Barrett worked on the government's flax-production programme and there is one report that she organised the flax factories which were staffed by women workers. In 1917 she was appointed to the board of governors at Swanley and in 1920 London University awarded her a doctorate. In 1922 she became principal of Swanley, commenting, 'I shall regard it as a life's work'. While she saw to it that 'students knew their horticulture and worked with precision and careful attention to detail' there is no doubt that one of her main qualities was her ability to steer the college (and the WFGA as it had become) through its financial difficulties. Twenty years after she herself was a student, she became principal with sixty-three students, a loan of £500, and an arrangement with the Board of Agriculture that a grant would be made on a pound for pound basis, up to a total of £10,000, later reduced to a half.

Throughout the Thirties, Dr Barrett (as she was always afterwards known) continued to work closely with the WFGA. A joint conference was held of all interested teaching establishments to encourage further co-operation and it concluded that there was a need for information regarding facilities for training, requirements for examinations by public bodies, and prospects for employment.

For her support for the study of issues of this kind, Dr Barrett was awarded the CBE for her services to horticulture in 1931 and in 1939 the Royal Horticultural Society's prestigious Veitch Memorial Medal. Co-operation with the WFGA also ensured that, since most Swanley students had membership, most were able to obtain posts on leaving college.

After a failed attempt to obtain university recognition through a link with the Bedford College for Women, Dr Barrett now approached Wye College for stronger university support, but despite the good co-operation which existed with this nearby institution, part of London University, the final merger of the two was further delayed. During the Second World War some college buildings were requisitioned, but these were badly damaged by German bombing in 1944 and the whole college was forced to evacuate. This facilitated the final merger with Wye in 1945.

Later in life, Dr Kate Barrett married her former lecturer Professor Richard Tabor, long after he left the college to join the staff of Imperial College, London. She died in 1977, aged ninety-two.

Chapter Eight

A Change in Direction

EVERY NOW AND AGAIN a comment is made which points to a fundamental change in direction, one which may have been there in the past but went unnoticed, though it was to be equally true for generations ahead. Such a remark appeared in the 1954 report of the WFGA, where, *à propos* of the first ever drop in the number of applicants for the Garden Apprenticeship Scheme, reference was made to a general lack of interest in the practical positions offered by the employment bureau. In part this reflected the growing mechanisation of both horticulture and agriculture, but it also represented the first intimations of difficult years ahead, with less activity in the regions and increased failure to interest members in running regional groups.

Throughout the 1950s there is evidence of a drop in women entrants into farming. Colleges began to waive the requirement for a pre-college year for the potential student to undertake practical work on farm or garden. Conference attendance was dropping and the President, Lady Nathan, speaking at the 1959 AGM, hinted that perhaps London University's interest in acquiring Courtauld House should be followed up. This remark was probably prompted by the fact that Miss Forster, the warden of Courtauld House, had resigned the previous year to start her own business in the west country, and the Council was experiencing the first of its abortive attempts to find a capable replacement: receipts from the clubhouse were also falling.

In the same year Dr Barrett had had to resign as treasurer owing to her husband's illness – though she remained on the Council – and her post was taken on by Miss D. Turner, an agricultural economist. (Here it may also be noted that the Association's accounting had always been under the direction of an all-woman team, headed by Miss Clugston. She had also been a suffragette sympathiser, and on retirement handed over to Miss Robins, the youngest partner in the firm, who continued to handle the accounts until the late 1970s.)

Despite these many problems, the WFGA retained its momentum. In 1959, the Association's sixtieth anniversary, the Queen Mother paid a second visit to Courtauld

A Royal visit for the Diamond Jubilee, 1959.

House, and there were three members in the 1960 New Year's Honours List: a CBE for Miss Tomlinson, and an MBE for Miss B. Havergal and Miss Mapledon Noakes. The financial position was difficult, but Lady Nathan had the right connections. Not only was her husband a director of Great Universal Stores (which no doubt made it easier for the Association to get a grant from its charitable body, the Wolfson Foundation, which gave the WFGA a grant for £4,000 over two years for educational projects), but she was also a governor of Girton College, Cambridge, and of Royal Holloway and

Bedford Colleges of London University. This was the kind of close relationship with the women's educational establishment which had always favoured the WFGA.

The following year, 1960, was a crisis year. Income from subscriptions and Courtauld House receipts was falling to a dangerous level. The organising secretary, Miss Crosland had to resign due to ill health and the hon. treasurer Miss Turner also resigned at the AGM after presenting annual accounts showing a deficit. Mrs N. Langdon, who had been a very able chairman for six years, reached the end of her term of office on Council in the year 1961 and was not prepared to stand again. An Extraordinary General Meeting was convened in October 1960 to propose raising the subscription to £2 per annum. The minutes of that meeting state 'the suggested subscription is not out of proportion to the change in the value of money and the

Lady Nathan, Chairman (left) with Mrs Langdon and Miss Crosland, Organising Secretary (wearing glasses).

facilities and amenities provided'. That certainly seemed to be the case, and once the urgency of the position had been fully explained the opposition was roundly defeated from the floor. However, a large number of proxy votes from absent members (mostly in Cornwall), who were less well informed, prevented the necessary increase at the time. Nevertheless at the AGM in April 1961, the Council made it clear they were not prepared to brook any avoidance of financial realism. Mrs Langdon, the retiring chairman, said:

> It had been discouraging for the Council not to receive a mandate for the increase of the subscription to a realistic figure for 1961, but letters from members in support of the proposal and the subsequent flow of voluntary increases early in the year had been encouraging. When the pattern for these increases had been defined, the Council had decided, and had instructed that this meeting be informed that, as from

Mrs M. Plume (centre), Miss M. Spinks, Hon. Treasurer (left) and Miss K.A. Murmann, Organising Secretary.

January 1962, the subscription would be £2 per year, except for those members who had joined in 1930 or earlier, whose subscription, on request, would remain at one guinea.

In proposing the election of Miss Spinks as treasurer it was noted that 'the treasurer has an unenviable task. A person of courage and determination is needed, someone convinced of the rightness of a forward policy for the Association'. In Miss Spinks, they certainly had that.

Temporarily, these actions offered a reprieve, but they provided no long-term solution and a mortgage had to be raised on Courtauld House. Selling the property was considered, but the cost of alternative accommodation was a deterrent at the time.

In the next two years the time of both the Council and their staff was too heavily consumed by money problems for any real development strategy to be formed. However the new organising secretary, Miss K.A. Murmann, had had strong links with education before coming to the Association and with her expertise, and the support of the Wolfson Foundation grant, the Association began to develop career and training projects. Within a few years it had achieved a reputation for disinterested careers advice in the agricultural and horticultural industry, and for years after it received a sufficient volume of enquiries annually from school-leavers, career officers and other bodies to justify remaining 'in business' during the long spell when its other services were in low demand.

In 1963 an offer for Courtauld House was received from the Society of Friends (the Quakers) with an option to lease back office and storage space on the premises. This option overrode the principal objection which had been raised to the sale three years before and the offer was accepted, with a good deal of relief from Council members, tired of coping with the domestic and financial problems of running a hostel in a greatly changed London. Times had changed and those who wanted accommodation in central London could now find it as cheaply in alternative clubs and elsewhere. The sale of the clubhouse enabled the staff to concentrate on its employment bureau and on careers advice and to put more effort into its conferences, which were becoming increasingly well supported. The Cambridge Conference of 1966 was particularly successful and set the pattern for residential conferences for some years ahead. These were also successful financially, the year in question showing a balance of income over expenditure of £400. At this time, too, there was continued attendance at career conventions, shows and meetings, where the future of farming employment was proselytised. There was support for two regional conferences a year. All these activities reflected well on the future direction of a professional body which represented what has been described as a 'lonely profession'.

The fortune of any small voluntary or charitable organisation is fundamentally dependent on changes in the social and economic scene in which it operates and which it is generally too small and powerless to influence – boom, slump, inflation, revolutions, wars sweep it helplessly along. From the mid-Fifties to about 1980 the Association, in common with many other small specialised professional and charitable organisations, was subjected to galloping inflation, government reforming legislation (often rushed through without thought for all the consequences), full employment coupled with the rising power of the unions, strikes, wage increases and bureaucracy undermining voluntary initiatives with lavishly funded government schemes.

The WFGA survived, where many of its contemporaries had to fold up, because it was underpinned by the capital fund resulting from the gift and sale of Courtauld House, but for many years its fortunes and activities were at a very low ebb. At one point there was a strong lobby in favour of winding up the Association and donating the assets to some other organisation with similar aims. The more conservative opinion, however, prevailed, namely that the Association had a duty to maintain the assets for the benefit of future women land workers, who, under different conditions, might once more need the help of a strong central organisation. This latter altruistic stance was made easier by the fact that no organisation with even remotely similar aims and objects could be found to be a worthy beneficiary.

The WFGA was not the only body dealing with women's farming training to suffer problems of finance and membership. The government withdrew its grant from Studley College in 1967, and it was closed two years later. Similar difficulties faced the famous gardening school at Waterperry. Miss Havergal retired in 1971 and her school was sold to the School of Economic Science the following year. Nothing so drastic was to happen to the Association, but there was a slow decline in both membership and

Miss Beatrice Havergal, founder of Waterperry Horticultural Training School (right), with student.

in activities. Rising inflation caused a 20 per cent increase in annual expenditure over two years and a less dramatic but continuing increase for years to come. This was not met by further subscription increases because to have introduced these would have been counterproductive, with members' wages always below the national average. As a result, the members passed a resolution at the 1970 AGM to the effect that 'the Association shall draw on its capital to a limited extent to be determined each year by the Council and Treasurer to [be used to] promote more vigorously the aims and objects of the Association'. Such promotion was necessary now that the activity at headquarters was much reduced. For example, there was a virtual standstill at the employment bureau because no women appeared to be actively searching for jobs in the profession. By 1972 membership had dropped to about 450.

The Association redesigned its leaflet calling it 'Join a Growing Concern', and made recommendations to such bodies as the Hudson Report on careers in agriculture and the earlier Pilkington Report on agricultural education. Inevitably its influence and

Waterperry students at work in the Rock Nursery.

scope of activities diminished over the 1970s. One example of this was that an *ad hoc* committee was formed at the height of the Cold War to provide guidelines for a new Women's Land Army if hostilities once more threatened. This led to a Memorandum on Pay Structure for the industry which was ignored by those authorities to whom it was submitted. However it formed the basis of a wages structure introduced some ten years later – without any acknowledgement of the work done by the WFGA.

At a more practical level, the Association's organising secretary moved to an even

Women who influenced the WFGA's post-war change of direction.

Miss G. Forster

Miss M. Chambers

Miss K. Herring

Miss B. Oakes

Miss J. Potter

Mrs J. Moullin

Mrs V. Fitzgerald

Mrs E. Cowper

Mrs H. Fovargue

Mrs S. Kurta

smaller office in Courtauld House, and then began working more and more from her home as conditions in London deteriorated. The Association had to face up to the fact that there was a change taking place in the background of the women who were applying for membership. This may to an extent have resulted from a change in education practices. Until the 1950s the Ministry of Agriculture was responsible for the bulk of agricultural training and the emphasis was on the practical rather than the academic. After the Ministry of Education took over, the pendulum swung the other way and the emphasis became more on the academic work, with, in consequence, a failure to turn out pupils with a practical grasp. This chasm between practical and academic training widened in the 1950s and '60s. Another reason for this may have been the personal background of the young women seeking training. On a visit to the Oaklands Farm Institute (home of the Hertfordshire College of Agriculture) for an annual conference in the mid-1970s, the point was made that in 1931 the majority of students had come from rural backgrounds and a high percentage returned to practical farming, yet now this trend was reversed and a far higher percentage, both men and women, came from urban areas. The 1977 Annual Report states that

> girls looking for careers in agriculture are finding it even more difficult to get the practical experience and training that is so essential for further education . . . [particularly] . . . during the usual practical pre-college year . . . This is the greatest hurdle and the number of establishments willing to take trainees seems to be diminishing, with farmers particularly taking the view that if they have to pay the same wages, they are likely to get more from a boy than a girl.

An Association survey of 1976 showed that, of about 400 girls interested in entering agriculture, only 40 per cent actually did so, with a similar proportion for horticultural aspirants. The figure for boys was better: of the 2,789 interested in agricultural employment, about 65 per cent actually began work on farms. All this went to the heart of the WFGA's interest in training. In 1978 the concessionary lease of office space at Courtauld House expired and Council decided not to negotiate a renewal, but to move the headquarters out of London, into the provinces where costs were lower and working conditions better. The first move was made to Essex, near the home of the then organising secretary, Mrs G. Calthorpe, and after her retirement to a rented office in Cirencester, Gloucestershire.

In 1980 the decision was taken to sacrifice some of the Association's 'cushioning' capital in order to undertake two pieces of research. The first and most important of these was completed by the publication, with WFGA support, of Dr Ruth Gasson's pilot survey *The Role of Women in British Agriculture*. This identified what women on farms actually did, and analysed the various groupings into which their activities could be identified. The Gasson Report was well received academically and by the farm industry itself. The second study was into the value of pre-college practical training, the lack of which had worried the Association for some time. Over 1,000 questionnaires were sent to newly qualified graduates, some of whom were now working abroad. The Association believed practical training to have a far greater value to would-be entrants than the various government schemes available, particularly the Youth Opportunities Programme, which they thought provided 'almost negligible' training. Not only that, but the YOP 'mopped up places originally available for genuine students . . . seeking to do their pre-college year'. The grim fact was that in 1981/2 the Association was only able to place two girl students in pre-college practical training. This threw the whole future of their career scheme open to question.

While the problem of practical training continued to preoccupy them, the Association remained active in what they called 'the field of equality for women'. An explanatory list of what this meant in practice was given in the 1982 Annual Report: the changing pattern of employment, a part-time workforce rather than a full-time workforce, greater involvement of women in public life, separate taxation for married couples, questioning the concept of 'work' against that of 'activity' and, of course, the long-lasting problem of equal pay. The outcome of these matters could, said the Council, have a 'devastating or exhilarating effect on women farmers'. The WFGA admitted in its report that they could 'in no circumstances be any kind of pressure group, nor had it any wish to be'. However, since agriculture was one of the most difficult of industries for women to work in, they must be up-to-date with current problems and opportunities. Certainly, they said, they continued to 'stand against any sort of positive discrimination'.

Alas, as forecast earlier, the government's involvement in training through the YOP and its successor the Youth Training Scheme, introduced in 1983, eventually brought about the death of the WFGA's pre-college practical training scheme. A direct result of the YTS was the disappearance of places which the Association's scheme had been intended to fill. The result was that a girl from an urban background who was offered a college place provided she first obtained experience by finding a job on a 'good commercial farm' could in practice find nowhere to go. Another example of the damage done by the YTS was its effects on the older student. A young woman who had stayed on at school to take O and A levels with a view to taking a degree course could expect no help from the YTS. The Association described the overall results of these government measures as 'critical for the future of the industry'.

One practical step which could be taken was to compile another survey, this time (1984) to ascertain the number of students who were obliged to find practical training, but who would receive no direct assistance in doing so from their colleges. The main finding of this survey was that, each year, over 3,000 students, of whom about 700 were women, had to find pre-college practical training for themselves. The Association put their findings to the Manpower Commission, pressing for these young people to be included in the Youth Training Scheme or to be otherwise grant-aided during their training year.

A major economy was brought about when, in 1983, Mrs Calthorpe resigned and the office was moved to Cirencester and a part-time administration was established, with voluntary input from Council members. This sufficed very well for handling the routine administration but with the improvement in external conditions noted above, the Association at last began to note a revival in calls on its advice and expertise, and could see projects that it could usefully undertake on behalf of its members and the industry in general. This added workload could not be undertaken without more staffing. While subscriptions and investment income would cover routine administration, the Council recognised that the Association needed, once more, the services of a full-time organiser, and in 1985 the decision was made that the salary should be drawn annually from the capital fund even though this would probably end in the demise of the Association eventually – 'better go out with a bang than a whimper'.

An abortive attempt was made to revive the employment bureau. At first this created considerable interest and an increase in membership as it was only open to paid-up members, but the service soon succumbed to the speed of the electronic age, with the best jobs and applicants being snapped up by 'instant' contacts, at the expense of the more cumbersome registration system. However, one valuable spin-off from the trial was that it identified a glaring gap in the provision of horticultural training. Increasing enquiries were coming in from mature women returners to the workforce, asking advice on how they could gain practical instruction in amenity gardening which would enable them to market themselves as professional gardeners within the locality of their homes. The Association discovered that there was absolutely no provision for training to fill this need. The idea of the innovative WRAG Scheme was born, though it was several years before it could be launched.

As the 1980s drew to a close, there was an increasing volume of enquiries about the profession; career packs with details of training programmes were sent out to appropriate schools and colleges. The Association also continued its policy of gathering information about the status of women in the industry. With the help again of Dr Ruth Gasson, now Senior Research Fellow of Wye College, Kent, a paper was prepared on *Farming Wives and their Status*. The results of this survey, published in *Farmers Weekly*, were produced in paperback as *The Hidden Workforce*.

One significant outcome of all this was the preparation and publication of the *Self Help Booklet* with contributions from lawyers, insurance brokers and the Social Services Department, explaining in simple terms the help available to women working in family farming businesses. While these initiatives were a hopeful sign of the continuing vitality of the Association, there was a tougher side, and this was expressed in graphic form by the treasurer. She had calculated that, to continue to run on the current subscription rates, it would be necessary to have a minimum of 1,200 members. In 1987, there were about a hundred new members and even this failed to bring the total to anything like that required. It was proposed to double the subscription rate to £10 per annum as an alternative practical measure.

In 1990 a small *ad hoc* committee was set up to consider the problems faced by mature women, looking for a career change as their families grew up, and interested in offering their services as self-employed amenity gardeners, to fill a perceived need in their home localities. While such women had no difficulty in accessing theoretical instruction in horticulture, through local colleges, correspondence courses, etc, there was no suitable provision for them to acquire hands-on practical training, which would give them the self-confidence to market their services professionally.

With experience of the Association's long-running apprenticeship and pre-college training schemes to draw on, a potentially workable and well thought out scheme was soon proposed and approved by Council, but financing it was a different story. For nearly two years the scheme was held up while every possible avenue of funding was explored, from local, national and European Community sources. In every case the project proved incompatible with funding criteria because it was purely practical.

Council felt strongly that to tailor the proposed scheme to fit the funding criteria would undermine its whole concept which was to provide a scheme designed around the needs of the trainees. Therefore it was decided to launch the scheme as it stood, with the aid, once more, of withdrawals from the Association's own capital funds, in the hope that this could be recouped by appeals to charitable funding bodies and other sources. Accordingly, a pilot 'Women Returners to Amenity Gardening Scheme' (WRAGS) was launched in 1992, and received excellent press coverage. It quickly became apparent that the Association had pioneered a much needed, innovative scheme, which has been acclaimed from all sides.

WOMEN RETURNERS TO AMENITY GARDENING SCHEME

The basic concept of the scheme is that trainees will garden for fifteen hours per week, for a year, in a carefully sourced private garden, within a twenty mile radius of their home, under approved and capable instruction from the garden owner or a head gardener.

The Association has appointed co-ordinators in each region of four to five counties to source and inspect potential placement gardens, interview owners and trainees and monitor the progress of the trainee by visits and contact during the year. Registration fees are paid by both trainee and garden owner and a training allowance is paid to the trainee.

To support the training scheme, the Association has developed a series of specialist one-day and weekend workshops to cover specialist subjects, arranged in different parts of the country.

The inauguration of WRAGS coincided with the appointment of Patricia McHugh as organiser. With her experience of charity fund-raising she could develop sponsorship for a number of Association activities including WRAGS. Initially the new scheme was restricted to gardens in an area within a sixty mile radius of Cirencester, now the headquarters of the Association. This scheme was not only unique, but the Council felt it was fully consistent with the aims and objects of the organisation and with the needs of the time. None of this would have been possible if the Association, reduced in numbers as it was, had not been operated on a viable financial basis. With the invaluable assistance of the stockbrokers who had managed the Association fund since the sale of Courtauld House, and with careful estimating, the treasurer succeeded in coming out, year by year, with a small but regular favourable balance with only an occasional annual deficit. The annual reports sometimes spoke of 'serious financial difficulties' but with hindsight these appear to be an over-emphasis on some temporary embarrassment. Income almost invariably met all day-to-day expenses. Somehow, if imaginative new directions were to be explored, there had to be an increase in membership above the magic 1,000 figure and yet this never appeared to be quite within reach.

The result of these financial restrictions was that staff shortages kept back initiatives and new ideas were delayed. In 1991, reporting on the publication of the *Self-Help Booklet*, produced in response to the previous year's survey *The Hidden Workforce*, the event was described as 'exciting'. But the attempt to produce a joint survey with the NFU on a replacement service for farmers' wives in periods of illness or absence, though described as 'an important achievement', fell by the wayside mainly due to a poor response from the farming wives. The following year, when all effort was directed to the WRAG Scheme, it was admitted that 'membership activities and other aspects of the Association's work have had to take second place'.

That year, 1994, there were over seventy new members. This is not to understate the success of WRAGS. In the same year six trainees had completed the scheme and a further sixteen were in placements. Those who had finished their training all found work. Standards were set high and it was interesting to note that a proportion of garden owners who applied to join the scheme had to be rejected because they did not have the training facilities required. In 1995 the number of placements processed increased over the previous year by 40 per cent and the following year the total number of trainees placed reached thirty-four. By 1999 it had reached and expanded geographically to a far wider area.

Parallel to WRAGS were programmes of workshops such as the 'Start Up Business Package' at London University and others with a more specifically vocational bent. A new development was the inception of garden tours around Britain and in Ireland and France, to view famous gardens, organised on a low budget basis. These were fully subscribed, made a modest profit and increased membership. This surged in 1997 when 200 new entrants joined the Association. Amongst other fund-raising activities was the sale of plants at rare plants fairs, paralleling the activities of the early members at the turn of the last century who had put their efforts into the sale of poultry, cheese and the like. In addition to this more traditional activity there was also an *avant garde* aspect with a survey designed to identify the type of computer systems to which rural women mostly had access.

However the hope of funding the development costs of the WRAG Scheme by money-raising appeals was not realised to any great extent. While some very welcome donations were made to the WRAGS Trust Fund, set up in 1993, they fell far below the administration and travelling costs that are incurred in running the scheme and it is proving impossible to develop it into more northerly and western areas, although the demand is known to be there. Once again the Association is being prevented by financial constrictions from developing its full potential and the life-giving and cushioning main fund is being rapidly depleted.

In its earliest days, the organisation had been urged to be international in its scope. The evidence is that this had always been more evident in the breach than in the observance – for good reason since agricultural conditions vary so markedly across the world. Despite this, the various Managing Councils over the years had made efforts to keep up relationships, however tenuous, with comparable bodies worldwide. As the Association entered the 1990s it reported that it had entered 'into closer contact with other professional and women's organisations'. This included attending the Conference of European Agriculture and affiliating with the new umbrella National Alliance of Women's Organisations.

The relationship which probably covered the widest field was membership of the

Women's Committee of COPA, Comité des Organisations Professionelles Agricoles de la Communauté Européenne. This body surveyed the high ground in Europe. Topics for discussion were the Common Agricultural Policy, Community regulations, equal opportunity for the sexes etc. etc. Within its ambit the Spanish Women Farmers' organisation planned a conference on 'The Role of Women Farmers in the World' and there were seminars on the 'Image, Role and Aims of Women Farmers'. WFGA delegates attended one or more of these conferences to represent the Association over a period of more than thirty years, and usually attended three or four meetings annually. The feeling has been that the effort was worthwhile and that 'considerable headway' was made. The value attached to the work of women farmers and horticulturists had been recognised in all EU countries, although some member countries did not practise what was legally defined. Much still had to be done for women in rural areas, particularly on the principle of equal treatment, including equal access to training and the recognition of professionalism on the family farm.

Those sentiments above echoed those which, over the years, the Association had affirmed in its declared objectives, and as those reprinted on p.156 show, they have changed little, over the years. True that in 1950 they spread to 'the British Empire', twenty-five years later merely to overseas and now, fifty years on, to 'Europe and throughout the World', but these changes merely recognised external realities and touched the cap of political correctness. The word 'professional' still describes the type of women to whom they appealed, and there is still, after a century, the same thrust towards education and improvement. The Association still believes that it must work with public bodies and must maintain 'appropriate international links'.

This stability of purpose is remarkable, particularly in relation to the change of management and location over the past fifty years. It is even more remarkable in light of changes which have occurred in the environment and particularly in agriculture. In October 1997 the agricultural editor of *The Daily Telegraph*, reporting on a London conference coinciding with World Rural Women's Day, wrote that women have:

come out of the shadows as 'the hidden rural workforce' and demanded greater recognition for their largely unsung role in the economy of the countryside. . . . Although women played a key role on farms and in other rural activities, they had been largely excluded (in past years) from policy-making bodies shaping the future of rural families and businesses.

Such words might have been written by Miss Courtauld or Mrs Wilkins, though they might have been surprised by the claims of one woman who spoke to the conference about diversification, stress, farm shops and business parks. The original WFGA women would not have been surprised, though, to learn that this speaker was the only woman on the NFU decision-making council. At a similar conference the following year the agricultural correspondent of *The Times* reported that delegates were told:

A new generation of 'land girls' is breathing fresh entrepreneurial life into Britain's flagging farm industry and is increasingly playing a management role once seen as a male preserve. Women are taking over the running of farms and injecting fresh business enterprise which could be the key to survival. . . . Women enrolling on agricultural courses now outnumber men.

The Association had played its part in this change, not only throughout its history but in the present day, for example, by holding no fewer than fourteen workshops in its centenary year on subjects ranging from propagation and organic gardening to basic landscaping. In the promotional material supplied to new members the WFGA claims that 'it has never lost the vision of its founders'. But that vision, although still wide, has a broader sweep.

With the runaway success of the WRAG Scheme and the current national obsession with gardening as a pastime, the organisation could be forgiven if it overlooked the fact that it is the Women's *Farm* and Garden Association. In practice, however, the Council of Management is not unmindful of its farming members and antecedents, though in the current parlous state of the agricultural industry it has been hard to see scope for its more traditional role in training and careers advice. In the early years of the Association's life there were more farming members than gardeners and it was possible for a woman on her own, or with a partner, to make a modest living from a variety of enterprises on a smallholding of some eight to twelve acres – poultry, pigs, bee-keeping, fruit and vegetables, perhaps some stock rearing. The loss of small retail outlets to a handful of huge supermarkets and processing chains has changed this scene and created in response the ever-enlarging agri-businesses of today, with an ever-diminishing workforce. But alongside this scenario, there is arising a small class of 'hobby farmers' – young couples buying up the farmhouses with a few acres that have been sold off after farm amalgamation and moving out from the cities to lead a 'greener' life and to rear their children in the countryside. There is a perceived need from them for some basic instruction in animal and land management at smallholder level, and as the Association moves into its centennial year the possibilities are being explored of a project like WRAGS to meet this need.

Both agricultural and horticultural members share a growing concern over the production of food, whether an allotment holder, a commercial grower or farmer. The demand for organic produce will grow and the debate on genetic modification will intensify and in response the Association has organised a conference to be held during its centennial year to discuss 'The Future Road for British Growing'. Members will visit both integrated and organic farms and see at first hand how farmers are balancing environmentally responsible farming with running a profitable business.

Career leaflets are constantly updated and continue to provide local government career offices, schools and colleges with information on land-based careers. This has always been an important aspect of the Association's work and with the diversity of courses available to students and with the qualifications expected by employers, this section of work has never been busier. Further support for students is the annually awarded travel bursary which is given to an applicant, male or female, young or mature, working on a project, either at home or abroad, which will benefit the industry as a whole. The Association also compiles information on other organisations who give out similar bursaries or educational grants and produces a leaflet which forms part of the career leaflet set.

Epilogue

Back to the Garden

THE FAMOUS *Oxford Companion* on gardening does not include a separate entry for women, though it might well have done so as many eminent women gardeners appear on its pages. Their names also appear in the records of the WRAG Scheme, details of which were given in the preceding chapter. Here is a selection from them.

One of the great heroines of 20th century gardening is Gertrude Jekyll. Although she was born before 1850, the bulk of her garden designing was completed from the Edwardian period through to the 1920s. In 1916 she was invited to become a vice president of the Union (later the WFGA) joining such other luminaries as the Countess of Aberdeen, the Lady Evelyn Ewart, the Duchess of Newcastle, Lady St Hilier, five professors from various universities – and others. Though she had no title, the Royal Horticultural Society awarded her the highly prestigious Victoria Medal of Honour. Jekyll was a singularly appropriate member of the Union as she was a fervent practical gardener who, up to her death in 1933, saw it as her duty to pass on what she had learnt to others.

'Miss Gertrude Jekyll's Boots', the famous painting by Sir William Nicholson.

In fact Jekyll had no formal horticultural training herself, having begun life determined to be an artist, studying at the Kensington School of Art and learning a great deal about colour from the painter Hercules Brabazon. Alas, her eyes troubled her so much that in 1891 she was persuaded to visit a prestigious eye specialist in Germany, and he discouraged her from continuing with all the things she liked doing best; obliged

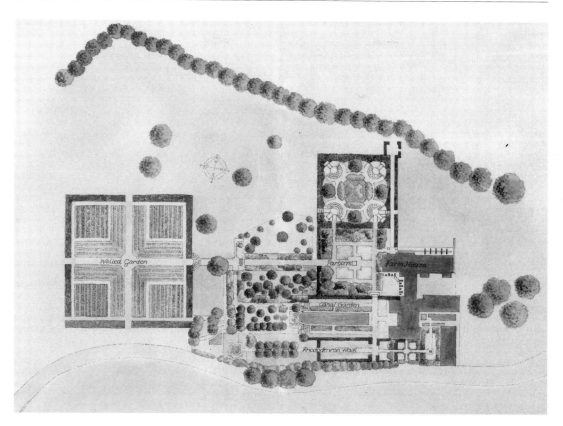

Plan of Folly Farm garden.

to abandon painting, she turned full-time to gardening, and, after 1900, to writing books about the subject. Her name is linked to that of the architect Lutyens (who called her his Aunt Bumps) and they created together some one hundred gardens out of his total of two hundred. Initially she was what Anne Scott-James calls the high priestess of 'the cottage garden cult', searching them for rare old roses and herbaceous plants. Later she became one of the best known pioneers of the herbaceous border. She would provide her clients with meticulous plans showing precisely where each clump of plants was to be located by their professional gardeners.

Thus, while she was an exponent of naturalism, her method of gardening was strictly practical, working almost always from planting plans. Later, when her fading eyesight no longer made it possible for her to visit her clients' gardens, she still adopted the direct approach – for example when commissioned at Hestercombe, Somerset, she would have small bags of soil sent to her home so that she could run them through her fingers and by 'feel' decide if it was suitable for the particular planting that she had in mind.

It was her example that inspired the horticultural training schools initiated by lady gardeners in the 1920s and '30s. Jekyll's influence came, also, to be more and more seminal in the style the British adopted for their gardens in the 20th century, an influence that eventually spread world wide. For example in 1917 she received a visit from Vita Sackville-West who adopted several Jekyll ideas for Sissinghurst, and some two or three years later Harold Nicolson is believed to have seen the plans for Folly Farm which her biographer Jane Brown says 'most beautifully express the interdependence of house and garden'. Another writer, Sir Herbert Barker, put her influence even more strongly. 'She had the power to see, as a poet, the art and creation of home-making as a whole in relation to life . . . its garden uniting the house with surrounding nature, all in harmony and breathing the spirit of its creator.' A third writer, Anna Pavord, says that the Jekyll style has today become the 'apogee of good taste'.

There is a direct line too, between Folly Farm and the WRAG Scheme in the 1990s, because it has been one of the gardens chosen for training. The original site was a farmhouse, as the name implies, and Lutyens added to this and to its barns. The first stage was begun in 1906 when he added a small 'manor house' in the 17th century tradition; the big barn, once thatched, is now tiled, and the areas between the buildings are lined by paths and archways to make 'walled courts'.

Another typical feature was a long herbaceous border – one of Jekyll's favourites. Jane Brown writes that Lutyens had asked Miss Jekyll's advice about gardens almost from their first meeting in 1889, and he would sketch out ideas as they talked over cups of tea at her Munstead Wood home. She was particularly fond of the courtyard gardens of Moorish Spain and these are said by Jane Brown to have been the inspiration for Folly Farm. In 1916, the then owners lent the house to the Lutyens family for the summer and Gertrude Jekyll was persuaded to come to stay here too; there is no doubt that the close knowledge of house and garden that the architect/gardener team thus acquired contributed to Folly Farm's almost unique unity of purpose. So by working at Folly Farm today, the WRAGS trainees have the opportunity of gaining experience in a garden that millions of people around the world aspire to own. It is nearly fifty years since the present owners came here, now managing the same seven acres under a head gardener who joined their staff as an under gardener forty years ago. Today, those inter-war years when the then owner employed a staff of eight gardeners seem a long way off. However the current WRAGS trainee, Sally Izett, explains that by training directly under the head gardener who has been at Folly Farm for such a lengthy period, working with a small staff dedicated to perpetuating the planting plans of the Jekyll era, she sees herself already as a member of a highly-structured team with clearly defined objectives. The head gardener Mr Honour is fully conversant with Jekyll's combinations of colour and structure and his trainee is slowly acquiring a little of his expertise in the herbaceous areas of the garden. 'It is early days yet,' says Sally Izett, 'because I work at Folly Farm only two days a week [the maximum time a trainee may work is fifteen hours a week]. But I can already see that not only will I have a clear concept of how to manage a large "estate" garden but thanks to Mr Honour's experience I hope to understand how a dedicated plantsman nurtures and brings on his flowers and makes the best use of cuttings etc.

'I should mention that at Folly Farm we gardeners provide flowers and vegetables for the house as well as looking after the garden itself and dealing with visitors who come to view the latter.' She adds, 'When I came here I had no experience of growing under glass, but the houses take a large part of the work schedule and I hope I shall gain experience which would be hard to come by elsewhere.' Sally Izett is not new to gardening, but she is making a career change, having found that what started as a hobby has now become a passion. She supplements her time at Folly Farm with a horticultural college course and hopes that in due time she will be able to become a full-blown professional.

Mr Honour makes it clear that Folly Farm is not really a garden for the present day. 'It's all hand work – that's the trouble. It's all laid out on different levels – you can't get machines on to it and everything has to be carted in by hand.' While nothing that has been done impinges on the Lutyens design, the changes in the labour scene have forced different approaches. The herbaceous borders at Folly Farm are not so wide as they were and the great lawn to the south of the formal garden is no longer close-mown several times a week. Sally Izett agrees that while in some senses she has become an aspiring museum curator rather than a creative garden designer, she feels her training has been no less a unique experience.

Not far from Folly Farm is Haseley Court, Oxfordshire, another garden which has had a great influence on what the British feel their homes should look like, yet a little later in period than the Jekyll/Lutyens partnership at Folly Farm. The house was bought by Nancy Lancaster, an American who came to England with her husband Ronald in 1926. They gardened at other famous houses they bought here, Kelmarsh Hall in Northamptonshire and then Ditchley Park, Oxfordshire. After her divorce, Mrs Lancaster saw Haseley in the 1950s and immediately fell in love with it.

Her biographer claims that she only feigned horticultural ignorance, and was in fact a practical operator of the kind she herself would have described as a 'dirt gardener'. On the other hand Sir Roy Strong is adamant that to the day she died she never lifted a finger in house or garden, though this is hardly borne out by her remark, towards the end of her life, that 'you only become interested in gardens when you are making them yourself' and 'the fun is really getting down flat on your stomach and weeding with your teeth'. Other reports say she thought nothing of getting out of doors at five or six in the morning. It is equally true that she had a knack of choosing the best experts to help her with any gardening problem which arose – Jellicoe, Norah Lindsay, Russell Page and Graham Stuart-Thomas are amongst those she called upon.

The then head gardener, Julie Worby (ex-Kew and also a WFGA member), explains the background: Mrs Lancaster had worked as an interior designer as well as a gardener and in addition to having a strong willed character she also had an extraordinary eye. The style she developed, however, was not at all intimidating – indeed Sir Roy Strong calls it 'elegant, unstuffy and informal'. Indoors, the world called it 'English Country-house style' and this soubriquet sums up the garden too. Some of its best known features she inherited – particularly the splendid topiary chess set which dominates the south side of the house, and is believed to have been there when the garden took its present form in about 1900. She also inherited the walled garden. The words are something of a misnomer as the garden is only walled in the usual sense to the south and west. It had previously been a kitchen garden but Mrs Lancaster decided to introduce an Italian-style order by planting tunnels of hornbeam to the north and

east. She also added a tunnel of labur-
num and, although this idea was not
new in her time, it has been said that
few have been executed with such
style and grace, for all the elements
are marshalled with stunning simplicity.

WRAGS trainee Rosemary Currie,
who trained at Haseley in Mrs
Lancaster's walled garden, notes that
when she began in 1993, Mrs
Lancaster was very much in evidence,
although she was then well into her
nineties. She had asked Russell Page to
produce an overall scheme, but she
found his ideas too fussy and what
exists today is very much her own
design. 'She was then living in the
Coach House,' says Mrs Currie, 'and
she would come out in the morning
in her wheel chair, taking a very
active interest in all that was going

Mrs Rosemary Currie at Haseley Court garden.

on. I remember in particular that sometimes if a plant appeared in one of the paths
she would be inclined to tell us to leave it there – things did not have to be one hundred per cent orderly.'

It has been said that she wanted the walled garden to appear 'a little sad' or the outdoor equivalent of what later became known in the interior decoration world as
'shabby chic'. This may have sounded romantic, but it did not come about by accident
or by any amateur approach; she knew her plants and passed on her knowledge to
other gardeners.

'I am privileged to have worked under her at Haseley, even if for only a fraction of
the forty years she spent there,' says Mrs Currie. 'She was always generous in inviting

people to visit her garden and ask for advice.'

Nancy Lancaster's obsession with 'hands on' gardening is also a feature of gardening at 'The Dingle', a family-owned nursery just outside Welshpool in Powys, North Wales. On a steeply sloping site, the owners Roy and Barbara Joseph have established a renowned nursery alongside a garden in the same four acres. Barbara Joseph served with the Land Army in Shropshire in the 1939-45 war. She joined after working on the Joseph family farm in her Cambridge University student days. After the war she married Roy Joseph and they settled down on sixty acres to farm a mix of poultry and sheep. Rather like Rosemary Verey, Mrs Joseph turned to gardening whilst bringing up her four small children. In 1968 the family decided to change over to horticulture and now their nursery covers both retail and commercial.

Today Mrs Joseph has little to do with the nursery. 'I just garden pretty well full-time,' she says. Julie Bucknell, the first WRAGS student to work at 'The Dingle', will be there for a full year, working in the garden rather than the nursery, because her aim, once her course is over, will be to set up a gardening business. On Julie's 'days' the two of them work alongside each other in the garden, tackling whatever needs to be done. In addition to the flower and shrub garden, there are two woodland areas, each planted as a memorial to one of the Josephs, and a small clay-lined lake.

Another nursery, Sydney Wharf, near Bathwick, Bath, North Somerset, is owned and run by Sheilah Hannay,

Nursery owner Sheilah Hannay's mother Jean on left, photographed with her sisters in their Land Army uniforms, during world war I.

whose mother served in the Land Army in the First World War. Sheilah was an advertising designer who moved to Bath. She began to propagate for her own garden and in 1984 opened the nursery. The current WRAGS trainee, Susan Green, notes that 'for many years this fine nursery has been known as "Hannays of Bath" and I have heard it said that its owners are "mad about plants". Not only do they embark on their own collecting expeditions to Africa, Asia and Eastern Europe, but their depth of knowledge – botanical and environmental – is remarkable. They are especially good on herbaceous plants and their wild forms. So as my own background was largely in vegetable gardening, it has been a very broadening experience for me to work alongside them.'

At Hannays, Susan Green does the normal jobs associated with a nursery – from selecting the seeds to the pricking out, potting and so on, with guidance and information from the Hannays themselves, noting the origin of a particular plant, who supplied it etc. etc. Because they are so enthusiastic about sharing their own knowledge with her, Susan feels that being a WRAGS trainee has broadened her interest and knowledge in a wide range of plants. She enjoys the nursery and meeting the customers, many from abroad, who are regular visitors to Bathwick.

North of Bathwick is the famous estate of Badminton, renowned for its annual International Horse Trials, but also the site of a fine modern garden within the environment of the old park. This was designed during the 1980s and '90s by the late Duchess of Beaufort who, with Russell Page in 1984, extended the garden on the eastern side of the house where old orangeries were already built. Two years later the Duchess, this time with François Goffinet, re-designed the garden on the south side of the house. Head gardener Richard Preest has worked with a number of WRAGS trainees, one of these being Penny Grist whose drawings here illustrate what she learnt about planting; work that the Duchess had completed; also what Richard Preest had been able to imbibe from the work of world-famous designer Russell Page who worked on Badminton's formal gardens shortly before his death in 1985. He is buried in an unmarked grave in Little Badminton. Indeed, this garden is a legacy of many of the great names of British gardening. The orangeries lead to immaculate matching box parterres in front of pavilions by William Kent (1685-1748) with clipped yews framing the vista to the park. Another influence here was Avilda Lees-Milne who lived in

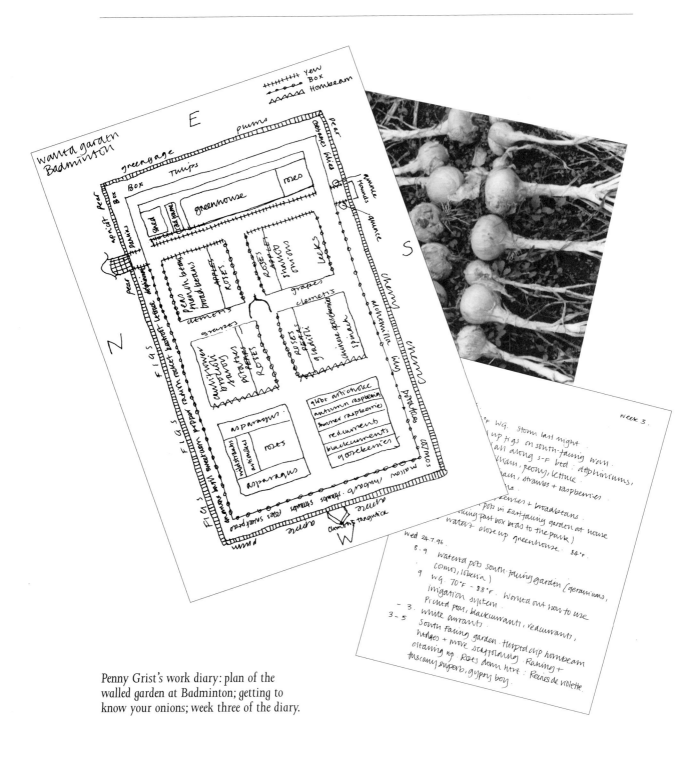

Penny Grist's work diary: plan of the walled garden at Badminton; getting to know your onions; week three of the diary.

nearby Acton Turville and Lady Westmorland at Lyegrove. All these gardeners left their imprint 'not only on the garden itself but on those of us who have worked here,' says Fiona Lewis, a former WRAGS trainee. There is a formality to working on a large estate, she points out, which is due to the requirements of the house for flowers and produce, far removed from the more relaxed organisation of the small unit. The former will have its office, its organisation chart, its distribution of responsibilities, its duty rosters, even its job descriptions.

Another trainee currently at Badminton is Elaine Flemons who spends two days each week on the estate coupled with a day at Lackham College where she is completing a design course. She came here from a completely different background – having worked for several years as a sculpture conservator for English Heritage. To date she has spent most time in the large walled garden where fruit and vegetables are grown for use in the house. The atmosphere is a disciplined one (the formality described in the preceding paragraph is standard practice at Badminton) and time will tell whether Elaine's future career lies as a member of an organised team or in a less structured environment.

The last in this pot-pourri of properties is very different from the others. Agreed, it was another 'hands on' site developed by the present owners, Peter and Jessica Duncan, who first saw it on a visit to Devon in 1984. It was then a working dairy farm with seven acres of pasture, but the Duncans set about a complete conversion, without much help apart from the availability of farm machinery. Kerscott House, near Barnstaple, appealed to Mrs Duncan because she had always wanted to make a garden of her own from scratch, one that began as an open field site, partly because her life up to that point had been the largely peripatetic one of a member of an armed services family. However she had spent several years gardening in Suffolk, where she was much influenced by Beth Chatto.

Starting from an intimate domestic garden near the former farmhouse, she set about a complete conversion of the remainder, partly from choice and partly from necessity. The latter came about because a major windbreak was required in this part of Devon, so a large scale tree planting exercise was mandatory. The beginnings of her woodland made use of mainly native trees, with plenty of shrubs and ground cover to give variety. A large lake and a bog garden were also early choices. Mrs Duncan does not work to a designer-type plan, but believes in the importance of a structured framework within which fluid planting schemes continue to evolve. In 1995 she read a report about the Scheme and took on her first trainee.

Mrs Duncan is enthusiastic about passing on her experience not only to a WRAGS trainee but also to garden society groups and other visitors, to whom she will gladly devote hours of 'talking time' each week. For example she explains to visitors that she had found an unusual way to plant up open spaces with a minimum of maintenance. 'I first decide on the vista and the views which I want to keep open, a decision usually dictated by the lie of the land, and I then plant my "backbone" of the bed I plan to create there. For the first two years this will contain only perhaps an ornamental tree and shrubs in mown grass, which, a few years further on, will be pulled together with an underplanting of ground cover kept in check simply by mowing. This way I can adjust the dimensions of the bed as the planting matures, yet the scale remains the same.'

At Kerscott House a living willow arbor provides structure to complement naturalistic plantings.

These descriptions of a few of the gardens and nurseries where WRAGS trainees typically spend their time in the millennium year have been selected mainly from workplaces in use in the WFGA's centenary year. They cover grand, historic properties as well as gardens where the background is rather work-a-day. As more and more women apply for places, the criteria for adoption may shift, but WRAGS co-ordinators will continue the search for gardeners who combine teaching skills and experience with an environment that will serve would-be trainees. The Association believes that it has forged a unique scheme here, enabling a wealth of highly professional experience to be passed on to a new generation of gardeners.

Objectives of the WFGA

1950	1975	1999
1. To promote and encourage the study and practice of Agriculture and Horticulture among women throughout the United Kingdom and the British Empire, and to further and advance the services of Agriculture and Horticulture.	1. *British Empire* deleted and *overseas* substituted.	1. *United Kingdom and Overseas* deleted and *Europe and the rest of the world* substituted.
2. To unite all professional women workers in Agriculture and Horticulture and allied subjects, and those interested in such work for women, into a strong central association.	2. No change.	2. *A strong central organisation* deleted and replaced by a *progressive national organisation.*
3. To help and advise in all matters concerned with these professions.	3. *Concerned with* replaced by *connected with.*	3. Added after *professions: and to keep members in touch with the modern trends, both technical and scientific, within the profession.*
4. To further the interests of women by seeking their due representation on public bodies concerned with matters relating to Agriculture and Horticulture.	4. To watch events and to make representations to public bodies relating to Agriculture and Horticulture, especially with regard to those affecting the interests of women. (These words appear in para 5 of the 1950 statement.	4. *To watch events* deleted and the following added after *women: and provide opportunities for members' views and concepts to be discussed and shared.*
5. To watch events and to make representations to public bodies relating to Agriculture and Horticulture, especially with regard to those affecting the interests of women.	5. To contribute to the welfare of countrywomen throughout the world by maintaining appropriate international links.	5. No change.

Glossary of Organisations

1. **Women's Agricultural and Horticultural International Union (WAHIU)**
   Formed in London in late 1899 as a result of the International Congress of Women held that year. The word 'International' was later dropped by the British organisation.

2. **Women's Farm and Garden Union (WFGU)**
   A new name evolved during the First World War from the earlier Union described above. The WFGU and WNLSC (see 4 below) were amalgamated after the war and renamed the Women's Farm and Garden Association (WFGA).

3. **War Agricultural Committees (WACs)**
   Set up by the government in the First World War on a regional basis.

4. **Women's National Land Service Corps (WNLSC)**
   Established by the WFGU to recruit and train women on the land in the First World War. Formed the basis of the Land Army.

5. **Agricultural Organisation Society (AOS)**
   Established with substantial government support to encourage the growth of farmers' co-operatives prior to the First World War, which later devolved into the National Farmers' Union.

6. **Women's Land Army (WLA)**
   Formed with government financial and administrative support during the First World War. Had similar aims to WNLSC (see 4 above).

7. **Women's Institute (WI)**
   A body established on the Canadian model, originally to organise work by women in rural areas, but which later evolved different aims.

8. **Women Returners to Amenity Gardening Scheme (WRAGS)**
   A scheme for trainees who are members of the WFGA to garden for 15 hours a week in a carefully sourced private garden under approved and capable instruction. Launched in 1992.

Further Reading

Adam Smith, Janet, *John Buchan* (London 1965)

Boyle, Tim, *Mark Beech: the Unknown Village* (London 1999)

Buxton, Dorothy (C.R.) & Fuller, Edward, *The White Flame* (London, 1931)

Cobbett, William, *The English Gardener* (London, 1996)

Ernle, Lord, *English Farming Past and Present* (London, 1912)

Gasson, Ruth, *The Role of Women in British Agriculture* (WFGA, 1980)

Gasson, Ruth, *The Hidden Workforce* (WFGA, 1990)

Jebb, Louisa, *By Desert Ways* (London, 1905?)

Jebb, Louisa, *How Landlords Create Small Holdings* (London, 1907)

Jebb, Louisa, *Small Holdings of England* (London, 1907)

Jebb, Louisa, *The Small Holdings Controversy* (London? 1909)

Lang, Theo, *My Darling Daisy* (London, 1965)

Lloyd George, David, *War Memoirs* (London, 1938)

Loudon, Jane, *Gardening for Ladies* (London, 1840)

Morrow, Elsa, *History of Swanley Horticultural College* (Wye, 1984)

Robertson Scott, J.W., *The Story of the Women's Institute* (Kingham, 1925)

Sackville-West, Vita, *The Women's Land Army* (London, 1944)

Sayer, Caron, *Women of the Fields* (Manchester, 1995)

Talbot, Meriel, *Land Girl, A Manual for Volunteers* (London, 1941)

Twinch, Carol, *Women on the Land* (Lutterworth, 1990)

Warwick, Lady, *Life's Ebb and Flow* (London, 1929?)

Wilson, Francesca, *Rebel Daughter of a Country House* (London, 1967)

Wood, Martin, *Nancy Lancaster and her Gardens* (Hortus, No.50 Summer, 1999)

Index

159